FLOYD CLYMER'S MOTORCYCLIST'S LIBRARY

The Book of the
NEW IMPERIAL

A PRACTICAL GUIDE FOR OWNERS OF
NEW IMPERIAL MOTOR-CYCLES

(COVERS S.V. AND O.H.V. MODELS FROM 1935 ONWARDS)

BY

W. C. HAYCRAFT, F.R.S.A.

SIXTH EDITION
1950

ANNOUNCEMENT

By special arrangement with the original publishers of this book, Sir Isaac Pitman & Son, Ltd., of London, England, we have secured the exclusive publishing rights for this book, as well as all others in THE MOTORCYCLIST'S LIBRARY.

Included in THE MOTORCYCLIST'S LIBRARY are complete instruction manuals covering the care and operation of respective motorcycles and engines; valuable data on speed tuning, and thrilling accounts of motorcycle race events. See listing of available titles elsewhere in this edition.

We consider it a privilege to be able to offer so many fine titles to our customers.

FLOYD CLYMER
Publisher of Books Pertaining to Automobiles and Motorcycles

2125 W. PICO ST.   LOS ANGELES 6, CALIF.

PREFACE TO THE SIXTH EDITION

IT is with pleasure that the author passes for press a new edition of this handbook, which has proved very popular among New Imperial owners. All lubrication and sparking plug recommendations have been brought fully up to date in accordance with those proprietary items now available. Also some useful advice on the care and repair of tyres has been included at the end of the book.

Owners of pre-war New Imperials are doubtless concerned about the question of obtaining new spare parts. Those in need of spares should be able to obtain what they require from Messrs. R. H. Collier & Co., Ltd., South Yardley, Birmingham, 25. (Telephone: Acocks Green 1681.) This firm undertakes rebores. Spare parts are also obtainable from Messrs. Claude Rye, Ltd., of 895-921 Fulham Road, London, S.W.6.

The author hopes, and is sure, that this publication will, as hitherto, continue to be of assistance in helping owners of 1935-9 models to keep their machines roadworthy.

This edition of *The Book of the New Imperial* should help and interest many thousands of riders who look after their machines themselves. Carburation, electric lighting, lubrication, running adjustments, decarbonizing, and general overhauling are all exhaustively dealt with; and if the advice given is put into actual practice, the owner-rider will be rewarded by obtaining maximum efficiency, quiet running, pleasurable riding and, last but not least, economy of upkeep.

W. C. HAYCRAFT

INTRODUCTION

Welcome to the world of digital publishing ~ the book you now hold in your hand, while unchanged from the original edition, was printed using the latest state of the art digital technology. The advent of print-on-demand has forever changed the publishing process, never has information been so accessible and it is our hope that this book serves your informational needs for years to come. If this is your first exposure to digital publishing, we hope that you are pleased with the results. Many more titles of interest to the classic automobile and motorcycle enthusiast, collector and restorer are available via our website at www.VelocePress.com. We hope that you find this title as interesting as we do.

NOTE FROM THE PUBLISHER

The information presented is true and complete to the best of our knowledge. All recommendations are made without any guarantees on the part of the author or the publisher, who also disclaim all liability incurred with the use of this information.

TRADEMARKS

We recognize that some words, model names and designations, for example, mentioned herein are the property of the trademark holder. We use them for identification purposes only. This is not an official publication.

INFORMATION ON THE USE OF THIS PUBLICATION

This manual is an invaluable resource for the classic motorcycle enthusiast and a "must have" for owners interested in performing their own maintenance. However, in today's information age we are constantly subject to changes in common practice, new technology, availability of improved materials and increased awareness of chemical toxicity. As such, it is advised that the user consult with an experienced professional prior to undertaking any procedure described herein. While every care has been taken to ensure correctness of information, it is obviously not possible to guarantee complete freedom from errors or omissions or to accept liability arising from such errors or omissions. Therefore, any individual that uses the information contained within, or elects to perform or participate in do-it-yourself repairs or modifications acknowledges that there is a risk factor involved and that the publisher or its associates cannot be held responsible for personal injury or property damage resulting from the use of the information or the outcome of such procedures.

WARNING!

One final word of advice, this publication is intended to be used as a reference guide, and when in doubt the reader should consult with a qualified technician.

CONTENTS

CHAP.		PAGE
	PREFACE	
I.	THE AMAL CARBURETTOR	1
II.	THE LUCAS LIGHTING SYSTEM	13
III.	NEW IMPERIAL LUBRICATION	23
IV.	OVERHAULING	44
	INDEX	102

THE BOOK OF THE
NEW IMPERIAL

CHAPTER I

THE AMAL CARBURETTOR

GOOD engine performance naturally depends to a great extent on correct carburation. All New Imperial models are sent out from the works with the carburettors carefully tuned and with jet sizes giving the best all-round performance. In the ordinary way it is not wise to alter the maker's setting, but sometimes it is necessary to retune the carburettor, when, for instance, the original setting has been interfered with. In this chapter the author has given full information and tuning instructions for the two types of Amal carburettors fitted to the New Imperial range. These carburettors comprise the two-lever needle jet carburettor and the single-lever non-needle carburettor.

The Two-lever Needle Jet Carburettor (all except Models 23, 25, 27, 30, 35, 37). This carburettor has been practically unchanged for many years, and the advice given hereafter applies to all 1935-9 models. In order to tune the carburettor intelligently, it is necessary to grasp how the instrument works.

How It Works. The carburettor is of the two-lever needle jet type, the mixture at slow or idling speeds being controlled by a readily adjustable pilot jet, whilst at higher speeds the mixture is controlled by means of a needle attached to the throttle slide and working in a restriction jet. The two-lever control must not be confused with the type of control that was used a considerable time ago on the two-lever carburettor, in which it was necessary to adjust constantly the air lever in accordance with the conditions under which the machine was running. This carburettor is for all practical purposes automatic, the air lever* being closed only to facilitate starting from cold. The carburettor slides are chromium plated to provide hard wearing surfaces.

Referring to Fig. 1, showing a sectional view of the instrument,

* On the 1936 Model 36 the air shutter is controlled by a knob on top of the mixing chamber (see page 11).

A is the carburettor body or mixing chamber, the upper part of which has a throttle valve B, with taper needle C attached by the needle clip. The throttle valve regulates the quantity of

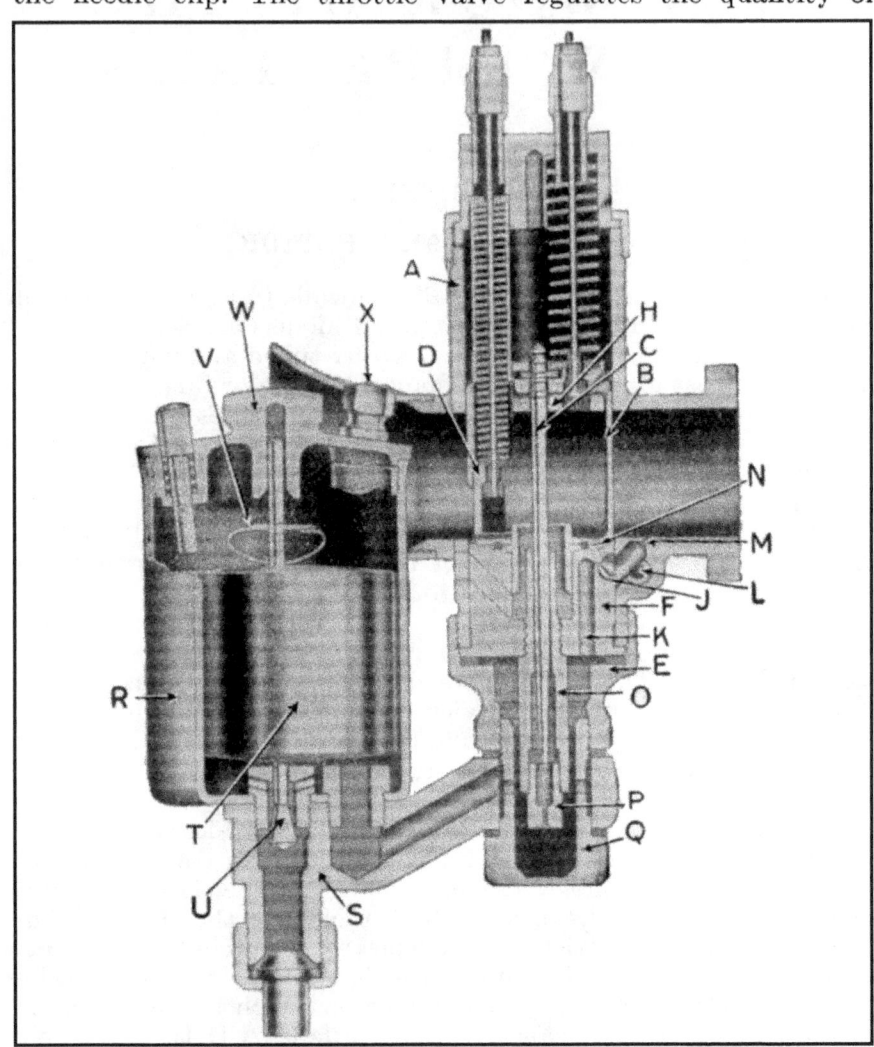

Fig. 1. Sectional View of Two-lever Needle Jet Amal Carburettor

mixture supplied to the engine. Passing through the throttle valve is the air valve D, independently operated, and serving the purpose of obstructing the main air passage for starting and mixture regulation. Fixed to the underside of the mixing chamber by the union nut E is the jet block F, and interposed between them is

THE AMAL CARBURETTOR

a fibre washer to ensure a petrol-tight joint. On the upper part of the jet block is the adaptor body H, forming a clean through-way. Integral with the jet block is the pilot jet J, supplied through the passage K. The adjustable pilot air intake L communicates with a chamber, from which issues the pilot outlet M and the by-pass N. An adjusting screw (TS, Fig. 1A) is provided on the mixing chamber, by which the position of the throttle valve for tick-over is regulated independently of the cable adjustment. The needle jet O is screwed in the underside of the jet block, and carries at its bottom end the main jet P. Both these jets are removable when the jet plug Q, which bolts the mixing chamber and the float chamber together, is removed. The float chamber, which has bottom feed, consists of a cup R, suitably mounted on a platform S, containing the float T and the needle valve U attached by the clip V. The float chamber cover W has a lock screw X for security.

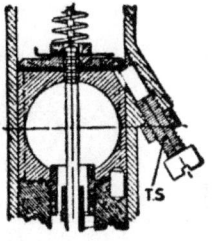

Fig. 1A. Amal Throttle Stop

The petrol tap having been turned on, petrol will flow past the needle valve U until the quantity of petrol in the chamber R is sufficient to raise the float T, when the needle valve U will prevent a further supply entering the float chamber until some in the chamber has already been used up by the engine. The float chamber having filled to its correct level, the fuel passes along the passages through the diagonal holes in the jet plug Q, when it will be in communication with the main jet P and the pilot feed hole K; the level in these jets being, obviously, the same as that maintained in the float chamber.

Imagine the throttle valve B very slightly open. As the piston descends, a partial vacuum is created in the carburettor, causing a rush of air through the pilot air hole L, and drawing fuel from the pilot jet J. The mixture of air and fuel is admitted to the engine through the pilot outlet M. The quantity of mixture capable of being passed by the pilot outlet M is insufficient to run the engine. This mixture also carries excess of fuel. Consequently, before a combustible mixture is admitted, throttle valve B must be slightly raised, admitting a further supply of air from the main air intake. The further the throttle valve is opened, the less will be the depression on the outlet M; but, in turn, a higher depression will be created on the by-pass N, and the pilot mixture will flow from this passage as well as from the outlet M. The mixture supplied by the pilot and by-pass system is supplemented at about one-eighth throttle by fuel from the main jet P, the throttle valve cut-away determining the mixture strength from here to one-quarter throttle. Proceeding up the throttle range, mixture control by the needle position occurs from one-quarter to three-quarters throttle, and from this point the main jet is the only regulation.

The air valve *D*, which is cable-operated on the two-lever carburettor, has the effect of obstructing the main through-way

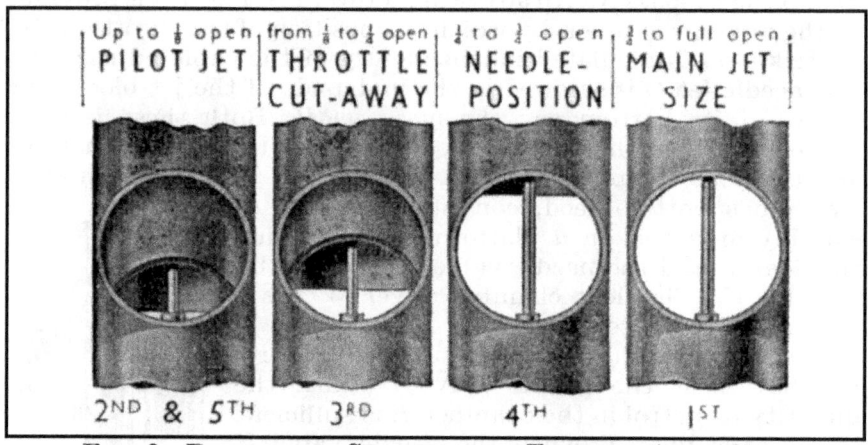

Fig. 2. Range and Sequence of Tuning—Amal Two-lever Needle Jet Carburettor.

and, in consequence, increasing the depression on the main jet, enriching the mixture.

Tuning the Two-lever Needle Jet Carburettor. Should the setting of this instrument not give entire satisfaction for particular requirements, there are four separate ways of rectifying matters as given herewith, and the adjustments should be made in this order: (*a*) Main jet ($\frac{3}{4}$ to full throttle). (*b*) Pilot air adjustment (closed to $\frac{1}{4}$ throttle). (*c*) Throttle valve cut-away on the air in-take side ($\frac{1}{8}$ to $\frac{1}{4}$ throttle). (*d*) Needle position ($\frac{1}{4}$ to $\frac{3}{4}$ throttle). The diagram (Fig. 2) clearly indicates the part of the throttle range over which each adjustment is effective.

(*a*) To obtain the correct main jet size, several jets should be experimented with, and that selected should be the *smallest which gives maximum power and speed* on full throttle.

(*b*) To weaken slow-running mixture, screw pilot air adjuster outwards, and to enrich screw pilot air adjuster inwards.

Screw pilot air adjuster home in a clockwise direction. Place gear lever in "neutral." Slightly flood the float chamber by gently depressing the tickler until fuel begins to escape from the mixing chamber. Set ignition at half advance, throttle approximately $\frac{1}{8}$ open, close the air lever, start the engine, and warm up. After warming up, reduce the engine revolutions by gently throttling down. The slow-running mixture will prove over-rich unless air leaks exist. Very gradually unscrew the pilot jet adjuster. The engine speed will increase, and must again be reduced by gently closing the throttle until, by a combination of throttle positions and air adjustment, the desired "idling" is obtained. It is occasionally necessary to retard completely the magneto before getting a satisfactory tick-over, especially when early ignition timing is used. If it is desired to make the engine idle with the throttle quite closed, the position of the throttle valve must be set by means of the throttle stop screw, the throttle twist-grip during this adjustment being rotated to the fully-closed position. Alternatively, if the screw is adjusted clear of the throttle valve, the engine will be shut off in the normal way by the twist-grip. Do not take the throttle stop screw out completely.

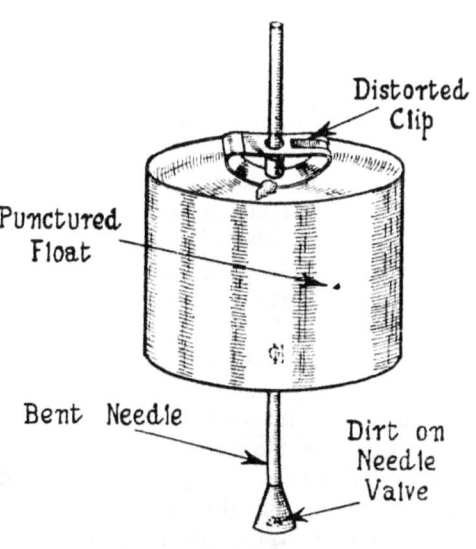

Fig. 3. Some Possible Causes of Persistent Flooding of the Float Chamber

(c) Given satisfactory "tick-over," set the ignition control at half-advance with the air lever fully open. Very slowly open the throttle valve, when, if the engine responds regularly up to one-quarter throttle, the valve cut-away is correct.

A weak mixture is indicated by spitting back through the air intake, with blue flames and hesitation in picking up, which disappears when the air lever is closed down. This can be remedied by fitting a throttle valve with less cut-away. A rich mixture is shown by a black sooty exhaust, and the engine falters when the air valve is closed. The remedy for this is a throttle valve with greater cut-away. Each Amal valve is stamped with two numbers, the first indicating the type number of the carburettor, and the second figure the amount of cut-away on the intake side of the valve in sixteenths of an inch, e.g. 6/4 is a type 6 valve with $\frac{4}{16}$ in. or a $\frac{1}{4}$ in. cut-away.

(d) Open air lever fully and the throttle half-way. Note if the exhaust is crisp and the engine flexible. Close the air valve slightly below the throttle, when the exhaust note and engine revolutions should remain constant. Should popping back and spitting occur with blue flames from the intake, the mixture is weak, and the needle should be raised a notch. Test by lowering the air valve gently. The engine revolutions will rise when the air valve is lowered slightly below the throttle valve.

If the engine speed does not increase progressively with raising of the throttle, and a smoky exhaust is apparent with heavy-laboured running and tendency to eight-stroke, the mixture is too rich and the needle should be lowered in the throttle valve. Having found the correct needle position, the carburettor setting is now complete, and it will be found that the driving is practically automatic once the engine is warmed up. For speed work on petrol fuels the main jet may be increased by 10 per cent, when the air lever should be fully open on full throttle. If extreme economy is desired, lower the needle one groove farther after carrying out the four series of tests described above.

Possible Causes of Bad Slow-running. If it is found impossible to obtain good slow-running by making the pilot air adjustment as described in paragraph (*b*) on page 4, it is probable that some defect other than carburation is responsible for preventing the engine running slowly at low revolutions. Air leaks are a possible cause which should be looked for. They may be due to a poor joint at the carburettor attachment to the cylinder and/or a worn inlet valve guide. Badly seating valves will also weaken the mixture. Defects in the ignition system may also be responsible for poor tick-over. The sparking plug may be oily, or the points set too close (see page 48). Possibly the spark is excessively advanced or the contact-breaker needs attention (see page 49). On "Magdyno" models, examine the slip ring for oil, and see that the pick-up brush is bedding down and in good condition. Also examine the H.T. cable for signs of shorting.

Maintenance of the Two-lever Needle Jet Carburettor. Periodical cleaning is necessary to maintain efficient functioning of the carburettor, and should be carried out in the following sequence.

Disconnect petrol pipe. Unscrew holding plug Q (Fig. 1) and remove float chamber complete. With box or set spanner, slacken the mixing chamber union nut E. Mixing chamber complete may now be removed from engine, simply by unscrewing the two nuts holding the carburettor on the induction flange. Unscrew mixing chamber lock ring, and pull out throttle valve, needle, and air valve. Remove main jet P and needle jet O. Mixing chamber union nut E may then be removed and the jet block F pushed out. If this is obstinate, tap gently, using a wooden stump inside

THE AMAL CARBURETTOR

the mixing chamber. Slacken lock screw X and unscrew float chamber cover W. Withdraw the float by pinching the clip V inwards, and at the same time pull gently upwards.

Generally it is sufficient to wash all the parts in clean petrol, but if the carburettor has had extended service, check the following—

(*a*) FLOAT CHAMBER NEEDLE U. If a distinct shoulder is visible on the point of seating, renew needle as soon as convenient.

(*b*) THROTTLE VALVE. Test in mixing chamber, and if excessive play is present it is advisable to renew this without delay.

(*c*) THROTTLE NEEDLE CLIP. This part must securely grip needle. *Free rotation must not take place*, otherwise the needle groove will become worn and necessitate a new part being fitted. *Be sure to refit the clip in the same groove.*

(*d*) JET BLOCK. If trouble has been experienced with erratic "idling," ascertain by means of a fine bristle that the pilot jet J is clear, and that the pilot outlet M in the mixing chamber is unobstructed.

To Reassemble. Refit jet block F with washer on underside and screw on lightly mixing chamber union nut E. Screw in needle jet O and main jet P. Open air lever $\frac{7}{8}$ in., throttle lever half-way; grasp the air slide between the thumb and the finger; *make sure that the needle enters the central hole in the adaptor top*. Slightly twist the throttle valve until it enters the adaptor guide, when on pushing down the valves the air valve should enter its guide. If not, slightly move the mixing chamber top, when the air valve will slide into place. Screw on mixing chamber lock-nut. *No brute force is necessary.*

Attach carburettor to the cylinder, pushing right home, and examine washer if flange fitting. Insert holding plug Q, and thoroughly tighten union nut E by means of a fixed spanner. Refit float and needle, holding the needle head against its seating by means of a pencil until the float and the clip V are slipped into position. Make sure that the clip enters the groove provided. Screw on the cover tightly and lock in position by means of the lock screw X. Fit holding bolt in float chamber with one washer above and one below the lug. Screw holding bolt into mixing chamber and lock securely. Clean petrol pipe and filter if fitted, and replace. It will be necessary to re-check the pilot setting if this has been disturbed.

The Single-lever Non-needle Carburettor (Fitted to Models 23, 25, 27, 30, 35, 37). A non-needle type Amal instrument is used on all 150 c.c. and some 250 c.c. lightweight models. No air lever is fitted, but a strangler device is included, this being incorporated with an air filter in the case of New Imperial machines. Control is by a knob which may be pushed in or pulled out.

How It Works. Referring to Fig. 4, the petrol tap having been turned on, petrol will flow past the needle valve P until the quantity of petrol in the float chamber G is sufficient to raise the float O, when the needle valve P will prevent a further supply entering the float chamber. The action of the float can readily be understood, for, as the quantity of fuel in the float chamber is used by the engine, the float O will drop, carrying with it the needle P, and admitting a further supply. Thus, automatically, the petrol level is kept constant.

In connection with the float chamber, it must be clearly understood that any alteration to the standard level can only have detrimental results.

The float chamber having filled to its correct level, the fuel passes along the passages through the diagonal holes in the jet plug H, when it will be in communication with the main jet D and the pilot jet C, the level in these jets being, obviously, the same as that maintained in the float chamber itself.

Imagine the throttle valve K very slightly open. As the piston descends, a partial vacuum is created in the carburettor, causing a rush of air through the through-way A, and drawing fuel from the pilot jet C. The pilot jet, being situated immediately beneath the base of the throttle valve, is subjected to a heavy depression, so as to obtain the necessary mixture for idling and small loads.

In the case of the main jet D, which is the longer of the two, and situated near the carburettor air intake, at small throttle openings it is inoperative, and the mixture is governed entirely by the size of the pilot jet.

The throttle K being almost closed, it will be seen that the pilot jet C is situated in an extremely restricted area. Consequently, the passage of the air from the main through-way will be restricted, and at the same time a high depression will exist on the pilot C. At this position of the throttle, it will readily be seen that not only is the main jet D shrouded by the throttle valve, but also the area of the mixing chamber in which it is housed is infinitely bigger than the area of the through-way exposed to the suction of the engine, in consequence of which no fuel is drawn from the main jet.

As the throttle valve K is raised, the area immediately above

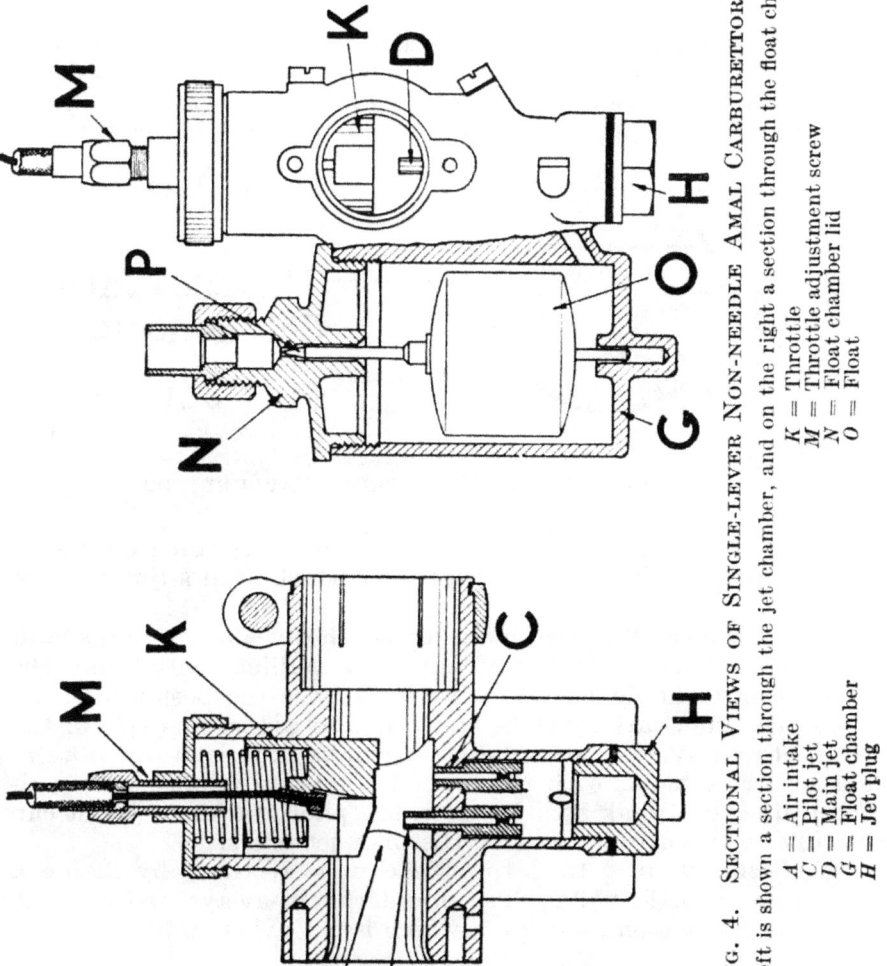

Fig. 4. Sectional Views of Single-lever Non-needle Amal Carburettor

On the left is shown a section through the jet chamber, and on the right a section through the float chamber.

A = Air intake
C = Pilot jet
D = Main jet
G = Float chamber
H = Jet plug

K = Throttle
M = Throttle adjustment screw
N = Float chamber lid
O = Float

the pilot jet C is increased, and in consequence the suction or depression on this jet diminishes, and at the same time increases on the main jet, so a balance between the two jets is obtained throughout the whole range. This briefly is the action of the carburettor.

Tuning the Single-lever Non-needle Carburettor. It is possible to vary the mixture supplied to the engine by three adjustments, which should be carried out in the following sequence: (a) main jet ($\frac{5}{8}$ to full throttle), (b) pilot jet (closed to $\frac{1}{4}$ throttle), (c) throttle

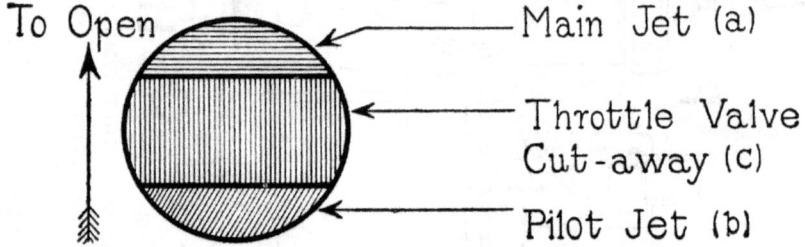

Fig. 5. Range and Sequence of Tuning—
Amal Single-lever Non-needle Carburettor

valve cut-away ($\frac{1}{4}$ to $\frac{5}{8}$ throttle). Fig. 5 indicates diagrammatically the part of the throttle range over which each adjustment is effective.

(a) Fit the smallest size main jet which gives maximum speed.

(b) This affects tick-over and slow pulling only, and the smallest size should be selected which gives the best idling. At the same time, care must be taken not to reduce the size of the pilot jet unduly, otherwise difficulty will be experienced in obtaining a correct blend with the main jet. If any trouble is experienced due to a weak spot between the pilot and main jet, it can usually be cured by increasing the pilot jet one size.

(c) Richness at $\frac{3}{8}$ to $\frac{5}{8}$ throttle can be rectified by fitting a cut-away throttle valve. The standard cut-aways are from O, which is flat bottom, to No. 5, which is cut away $\frac{5}{16}$ in.

Maintenance of Single-lever Non-needle Carburettor. To maintain the efficiency of the carburettor, you are strongly advised to periodically clean it. This is best done by entirely dismantling and washing each part in clean petrol. Renew any worn parts, such as the needle valve, if head has a distinct ridge at the point of seating; the throttle valve, if excessive side play is present; the mixing chamber union nut washer, if worn or damaged. See that filter is clean.

When reassembling, no brute force is necessary. Make sure that the needle valve enters top of the float chamber cover easily; that the mixing chamber is fitted vertically and pushed right home on engine stub; that the washer is good, if flange fitting to cylinder; that the jets are fitted in their correct places.

Position of Controls for Starting. In the case of machines having a two-lever needle jet carburettor, close the air lever completely, open the throttle about one-eighth of its total movement by turning the twist-grip *inwards* and set the ignition lever at three-quarters full advance. Where coil ignition is fitted, switch on the ignition by means of the ignition key and note that the red warning lamp at the back of the ammeter shows. When the engine starts, gradually open the air lever until it is fully opened. Also advance the ignition lever fully.

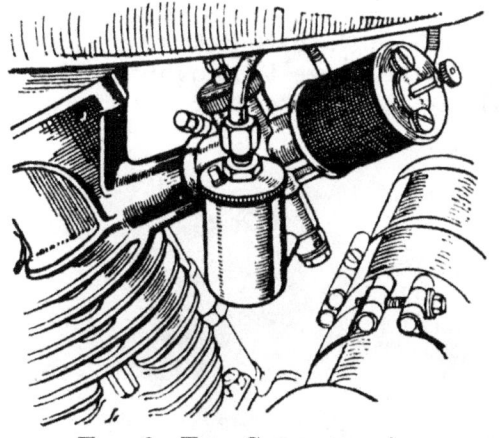

Fig. 6. The Combined Air Strangler and Filter
Used in conjunction with the single-lever non-needle carburettor.

On the 1936 Model 36 with "Magdyno" ignition, the air slide is actuated by means of a knob on top of the mixing chamber. To shut off the air supply for starting up, turn the knob *clockwise* and at the same time push the knob inwards. Immediately the engine starts, gradually pull out the knob and simultaneously turn it *anti-clockwise* until the spring clip can be felt engaging a slot. In this position the air control is fully opened. The object of the spring clip and slot is to prevent vibration, causing the control to close while riding.

With machines having a single-lever non-needle carburettor, to start up, close the air strangler by pressing in the knob on the air filter (see Fig. 6), open the throttle about one-eighth of its full movement by turning the twist-grip *inwards*, and set the ignition lever at three-quarters' full advance. On coil ignition models do not forget to switch on the ignition by turning the key until the warning lamp shows red. When the engine fires, open the air strangler gradually until it is fully open by pulling the knob as far as it will go. On "Maglita" models there is no ignition switch.

Note that on all models the carburettor should be flooded

slightly when starting from cold, but this should not be done when the engine is warm. Always keep the throttle nearly closed when starting, as this induces a high velocity air stream over the pilot jet. Keep both ignition and air levers wide open while actually riding, and do not forget on coil ignition models to switch off the ignition when leaving the machine stationary. If this is not done, the battery may become run down.

To Clean Air Filter (Single-lever Non-needle Carburettor). Unscrew both of the nuts at the end of the air filter and detach the filter from the carburettor. To remove impurities from the filter, wash the gauze thoroughly in clean petrol. Afterwards replace the combined filter and strangler on the carburettor.

CHAPTER II

THE LUCAS LIGHTING SYSTEM

LUCAS electrical equipment is specified exclusively on 1935 models onwards. The equipment used includes (*a*) a "Magdyno," (*b*) a coil ignition set, or (*c*) a "Maglita." In this chapter it is the author's intention to deal with these three types of equipment, together with the batteries and lamps. Components concerned solely with ignition (such as, for example, the contact-breaker) are dealt with in Chapter IV. On coil ignition models the Lucas dynamo is similar to the dynamo portion of the "Magdyno," and the same maintenance instructions apply in both cases. Compensated voltage control is provided on all 1937 and later dynamos.

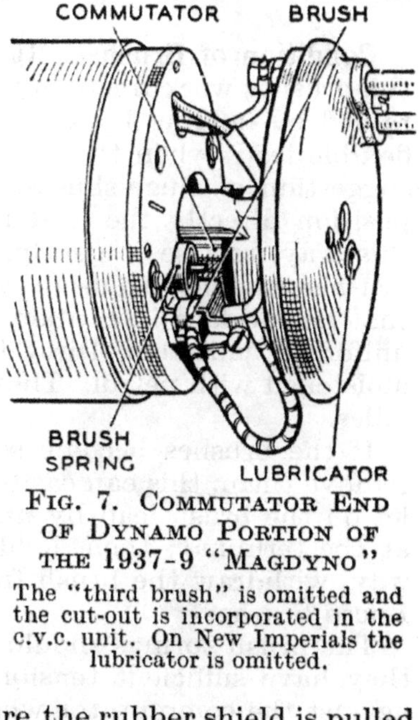

DYNAMO MAINTENANCE

Before removing the cover for any reason, it is necessary to disconnect the positive lead of the battery to avoid the danger of reversing the polarity of the dynamo or short-circuiting the battery, either of which might cause serious damage. To disconnect, remove the rubber shield and unscrew the cable connector, being careful not to touch the frame with the cable and cause a short circuit. When reconnecting, make sure the rubber shield is pulled well over the connector.

FIG. 7. COMMUTATOR END OF DYNAMO PORTION OF THE 1937-9 "MAGDYNO"

The "third brush" is omitted and the cut-out is incorporated in the c.v.c. unit. On New Imperials the lubricator is omitted.

If at any time a "Magdyno" or coil ignition model *without compensated voltage control* is ridden with the battery disconnected, or in any way out of service, it is essential to run with the switch in the "OFF" position. In the case of "Magdyno," coil ignition models *with compensated voltage control*, it is possible to run with the battery removed or disconnected without causing damage to the equipment. Such running, however, should only be undertaken in an emergency, and it should be noted that with coil ignition models a running start will probably be necessary.

With the "Maglita" the lamps, in case of emergency, can be run direct off the generator by disconnecting the battery and turning the control switch to the "H" position. Under these circumstances, the engine speed should be kept down below about 2500 r.p.m., as otherwise the lamps may burn out. Never run the generator direct with the switch in the "L" position, as this is likely to burn out both the pilot and tail bulbs. If direct running is necessary, put the control switch to full "on" either before starting up or while the engine is turning over very slowly. Always turn the control switch to the "off" position after stopping the engine, as this prevents the possible discharging of the battery in the event of the cut-out sticking.

Condition of Brushes. It is very important to make sure that the brushes work freely in their holders. This can be easily ascertained by holding back the spring lever and gently pulling each flexible lead, when the brush should move without the slightest suggestion of sluggishness. It should also return to its original position directly the lead is let go. When testing the brush in this way, release it gently, otherwise it may get chipped. The brushes should be clean and "bed" over the whole surface; that is, the face in contact with the commutator should appear uniformly polished. Dirty brushes may be cleaned with a cloth moistened with petrol. They should be inspected every 3000-4000 miles.

If the brushes become so badly worn that it is necessary to remove them, this can easily be done as follows: Release the eyelet on the brush lead by unscrewing the hexagonal nut or screw at the terminal; then, holding back the spring lever out of the way, withdraw the brush from its holder. Replace with genuine Lucas brushes.

The brush springs should be inspected occasionally to see that they have sufficient tension to keep the brushes firmly pressed against the commutator when the machine is running. It is particularly necessary to keep this in mind when the brushes have been in use a long time and are very much worn down. Owners are cautioned that it is unwise to insert brushes of a grade other than that supplied with the machine, or to change the tension springs. The arrangement provided has been made only after many years' experience, and will be found to give the best results and the longest life. It is really best when the brushes become so worn that they no longer bed down on the commutator, to go to a Lucas Service Depot, as this ensures the brushes being properly "bedded."

THE LUCAS LIGHTING SYSTEM

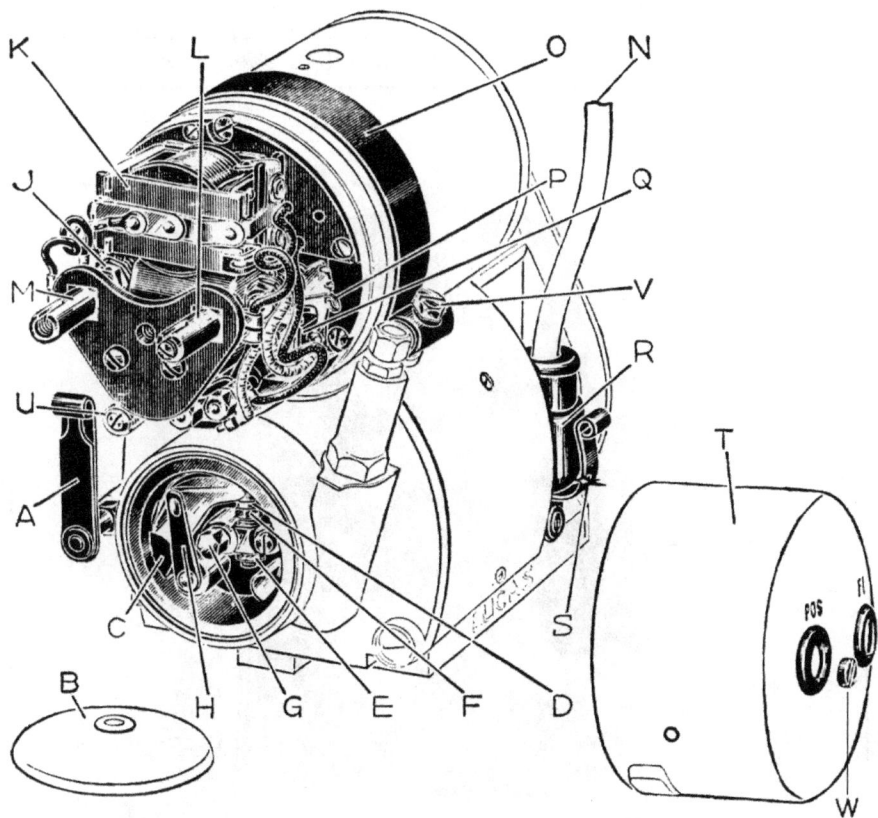

Fig. 8. 1935-6 Lucas "Magdyno" with Cut-out and "Third Brush"

A = Securing spring for contact-breaker cover
B = Contact-breaker cover
C = Fibre heel
D = Contact points
E = Locking nut
F = Adjustable contact point
G = Contact-breaker fixing screw
H = Locating spring
J = Nut securing brush eyelet
K = Cut-out
L = Terminal marked "F1"
M = Terminal marked "POS"
N = Cable to sparking plug
O = Dynamo securing strap
P = Spring lever holding brush in position
Q = Carbon brush
R = H.T. pick-up
S = Securing spring for pick-up
T = Commutator end-cover
U = Earthing terminal
V = Screw securing dynamo strap
W = Cover fixing screw

16 BOOK OF THE NEW IMPERIAL

Commutator Maintenance. The surface of the commutator should be kept clean and free from oil or brush dust, etc. Should any grease or oil work its way on to the commutator through over-lubrication, it will not only cause sparking, but, in addition, carbon and copper dust will be collected in the grooves between

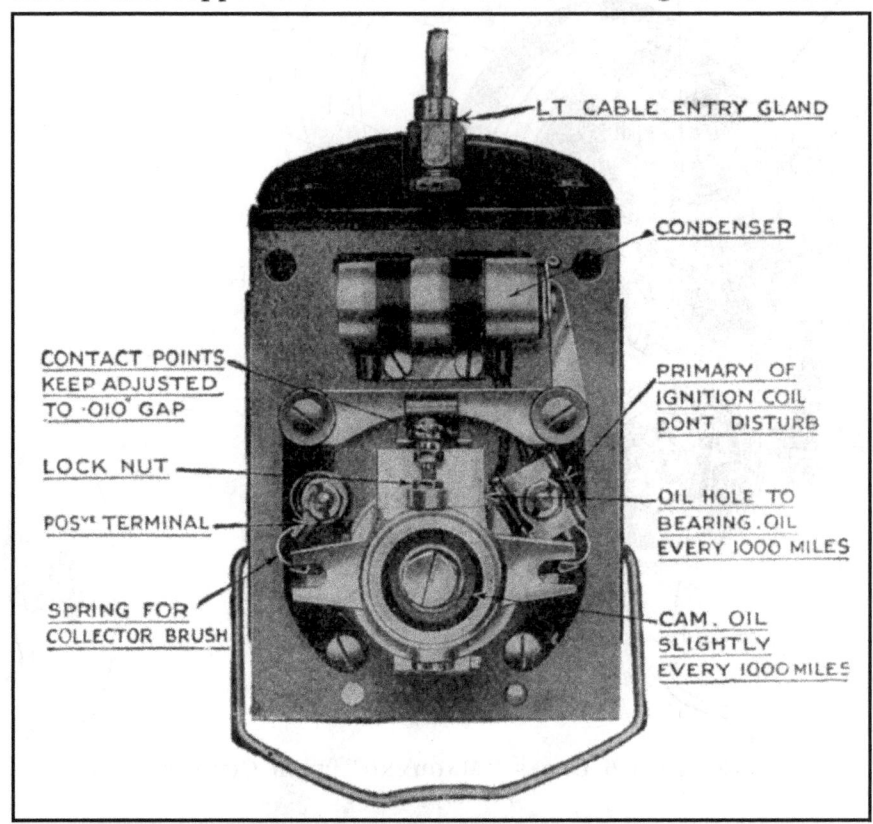

Fig. 9. Contact-breaker Side of Lucas "Maglita" Showing Some Maintenantce Points
(*Joseph Lucas, Ltd.*)

the commutator segments. The best way to clean the commutator is, without disconnecting any leads, to remove from its box one of the main brushes and, inserting a fine duster in the box, hold it, by means of a suitably-shaped piece of wood, against the commutator surface, causing the armature to be rotated at the same time. If the commutator has been neglected for long periods, it may have become blackened. To clean a badly blackened commutator, press (with a piece of wood) fine glass-paper against the segments while rotating the armature. Afterwards blow out all dust particles with a tyre pump. If the segments are highly polished and of a *dark bronze* colour, leave them alone.

The Cut-out. This, on "Magdyno" and coil ignition models minus compensated voltage control, is mounted on the dynamo end bracket and constitutes an automatic switch whose duty it is to prevent the battery discharging into the dynamo when the engine is running slowly or is stationary. When the voltage at the dynamo exceeds the battery voltage as the engine is accelerated, the cut-out contacts close, and when the speed is reduced and the battery voltage exceeds the dynamo voltage the contacts open, so making it absolutely impossible for the battery to discharge back through the dynamo. It should be noted, however, that the cut-out is not intended to and cannot prevent over-charging of the battery. Compensated voltage control, however, does prevent over-charging.

If by any unlucky chance the dynamo polarity becomes reversed, the remedy is to run the engine *slowly* with the switch in the "C" position and then press the cut-out contacts together momentarily. In the case of the Lucas "Maglita" (Fig. 9), the cut-out is contained in a circular case forming part of the armature spindle, and has a centrifugal type of control.

Concerning Compensated Voltage Control. The C.V.C. unit (1937 onwards) comprises the cut-out and voltage control (working on the trembler principle) neatly housed in a box on the machine. It is connected across the brushes and sees to it that the battery is kept properly charged automatically, the dynamo output varying according to the state of charge of the battery and the load. The regulator begins to operate when the dynamo voltage reaches about 7·3 volt. With this equipment the "third brush" is omitted and there are only three switch positions—"Off," "L," and "H." In all three positions the dynamo gives a controlled output, thus relieving the rider of much responsibility. During daylight running, when the battery is well charged, the ammeter may indicate a charge of only 1 or 2 amperes, for the dynamo gives only a trickle charge. This may occur with the switch "Off." If the battery is low, the ammeter may show 6 amp. The voltage control unit is sealed by the makers and should not be tampered with, the only likely trouble being oxidizing or welding together of the contacts (see Fig. 10) due to accidental crossing of the dynamo field and positive leads. If a "Lucas-Knife" battery is fitted, the regulator should be changed at a Lucas Service Depot. Excellent service is given at Lucas depots, and the reader is advised to call at one whenever any spot of bother is encountered in regard to the electrical equipment.

Keep the battery connexions clean and tight, otherwise the ammeter readings will suggest a fully-charged battery when such is not the case. Also do not neglect a badly discharged battery. See that the dynamo to regulator cable insulations are sound and that the connexions are good. The earth contact of the regulator must also be perfect.

What the Ammeter Does. This centre-zero instrument, which shows a charge on one side and a discharge on the other, is provided to give a reading of the amount of current flowing to and

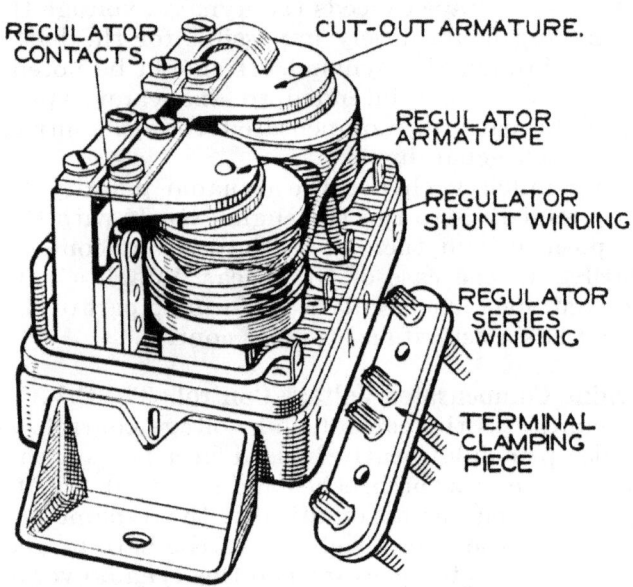

FIG. 10. COMPENSATED VOLTAGE CONTROL UNIT WITH LID REMOVED, SHOWING CUT-OUT AND REGULATOR
Note the "trembler" contact-breaker on the left.
(*Joseph Lucas, Ltd.*)

from the battery. It indicates whether or not the electrical equipment is functioning satisfactorily.

Absence of Fuses. In order to simplify the system as far as possible, no fuse is provided. If all the connexions are kept clean and tight, there is no possibility of any excess current causing damage to the equipment.

Lucas Dynamo Terminals. The positive dynamo terminal, marked "POS," and the shunt-field terminal, marked "FI," are situated on either side of the cover (Fig. 8). To connect up, the

THE LUCAS LIGHTING SYSTEM

cables merely have to be bared and clamped in their terminals by means of grub-screws.

On the 1937-9 generator (Fig. 7) with separate voltage control unit, the positive dynamo terminal is marked "D" and the shunt-field terminal "F" on the cover. To connect up, first slacken the fixing screw on the terminal block and remove the clamping plate. Then withdraw the metal sleeve from each terminal. The cables should then be passed through the clamping plate holes and bared at the ends for ⅜ in. Now fit the sleeves over the cables, bend back the wires over them and push the sleeves home into the terminals, finally screwing down the clamping plate.

CARE OF THE BATTERY (LEAD-ACID TYPE)

It is of the utmost importance that the battery should receive regular attention to keep it in good condition.

The following are the most important maintenance hints—

1. Keep the acid level with the tops of the separators.
2. Add only distilled water, never tap water.
3. Test the condition of the battery by taking readings of the specific gravity of the acid with a hydrometer.
4. The battery must never be left in a discharged condition.

Topping Up. Examine the acid level about once a month, and even more frequently in hot weather and tropical climates. Be careful not to hold a naked light near the vent holes. If the level is below the tops of the separators, add distilled water as required. This should be added just before a charge run, as the agitation due to running and the gassing will thoroughly mix the solution. If the solution has been spilled by accident, add diluted sulphuric acid of specific gravity equal to that in the remaining cells. When the inspection is carried out, hydrometer readings (specific gravity values) should be taken of the solution in one of the cells, and occasionally of that in all the cells; the reading for each cell should be the same. These readings are the most reliable method of indicating accurately the condition of the cells. Keep the battery connexions clean and free from acid. Smear well with petroleum jelly to prevent corrosion.

Charging Hints. The amount of charging on machines without compensated voltage control varies considerably owing to various running conditions. If the light is poor and falls off when the machine is standing, charging should be immediately carried out. It is difficult to lay down rigid instructions on the question of charging, since it largely depends upon the extent to which the lamps are used. With the coil ignition models more charging is necessary than with the magneto ignition models, since the current is used for ignition and lighting. The following suggestion may serve as a rough guide: leave the switch in the "charge" position during the day for about 50 per cent of the night riding (a slight charge should flow to the battery when running with lamps on). Charging a battery after discharge raises the specific gravity, and discharging lowers the specific gravity. Place on charge, either by running the engine or using an independent electrical supply, immediately any battery whose specific gravity has fallen as low as 1·210. Take hydrometer readings whenever trouble is experienced with any part of the electrical system. *The correct specific gravity reading is* 1·280–1·300 for Lucas batteries fully charged, about 1·210 for batteries half discharged, and below 1·150 fully discharged (at 60°, F.).

Storage. If the equipment is laid by for several months, the battery must be given a small charge from a separate source of electrical energy about once a fortnight, in order to obviate any permanent sulphation of the plates. In no circumstances must the electrolyte be removed from the battery and the plates allowed to dry, as certain chemical changes take place which result in permanent loss of capacity.

LUCAS LAMPS

The DU Type Headlamp. This lamp, used on New Imperials from 1935 onwards, is fitted with a double filament bulb, the one filament providing the normal driving light, while the second one gives an anti-dazzle dipped beam. The change over from the normal driving light to the dipped beam is made by a handlebar switch. A small pilot bulb is provided for use when the machine is stationary or when driving in town. An ammeter is incorporated at the back of the lamp.

Switch Positions. The lighting switch housed on the back of the lamp, or instrument panel on some 1935 models, has the following positions—

"Off"—Lamps off, and dynamo not charging.

"C"—Lamps off and dynamo giving half its normal output.

"H"—Headlamp (driving light), tail lamp, and sidecar lamp (when fitted) on; dynamo or "Maglita" giving maximum output, 4–5 amp. "Magdyno," 3½ amp. "Maglita."

"L"—With the exception that the pilot light is in the place of the driving light, the conditions are exactly the same as in position "H." On 1937–9 "Magdyno" and coil ignition models the "C" position is omitted (page 17) and the dynamo can charge in *all* switch positions.

THE LUCAS LIGHTING SYSTEM 21

How to Adjust Focus (Lucas Headlamps). To focus the main bulb, it is necessary to remove the lamp front and reflector by pressing back the fixing clip. Then slacken the clamping screw which secures the bulb-holder and move the bulb-holder and bulb until correct focus is obtained. Afterwards tighten the clamping screw. To remove the bulb-holder it is only necessary to press back the two securing springs. When replacing the lamp front and reflector, the top of the rim should be located first.

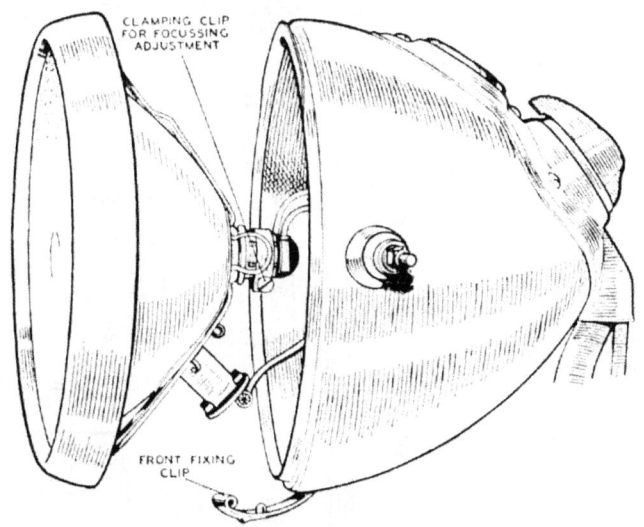

Fig. 11. Lucas Du Type Headlamp Incorporating Ammeter and Lighting Switch

On coil ignition models an ignition key is fitted in the centre of the switch.

Replacement of Lucas Bulbs. When the replacement of any bulb is necessary, genuine Lucas bulbs should be used. The filaments are arranged to be in focus, and give the best results with Lucas reflectors. When it is found necessary to replace the main headlamp bulb, see that the bulb is fitted the correct way round, i.e. with the dipped beam filament above the centre filament. Always focus the headlamp after fitting a new bulb.

The number of the bulb for the headlamp driving and dipped beam light is 70 (except on "Maglita" models, when it is 68, and coil models, when it is 69); and that of the headlamp pilot, sidecar, panel, and tail lights, 200. Bulbs Nos. 70, 68, 69 are of 24 watt, 12 watt, and 18 watt respectively.

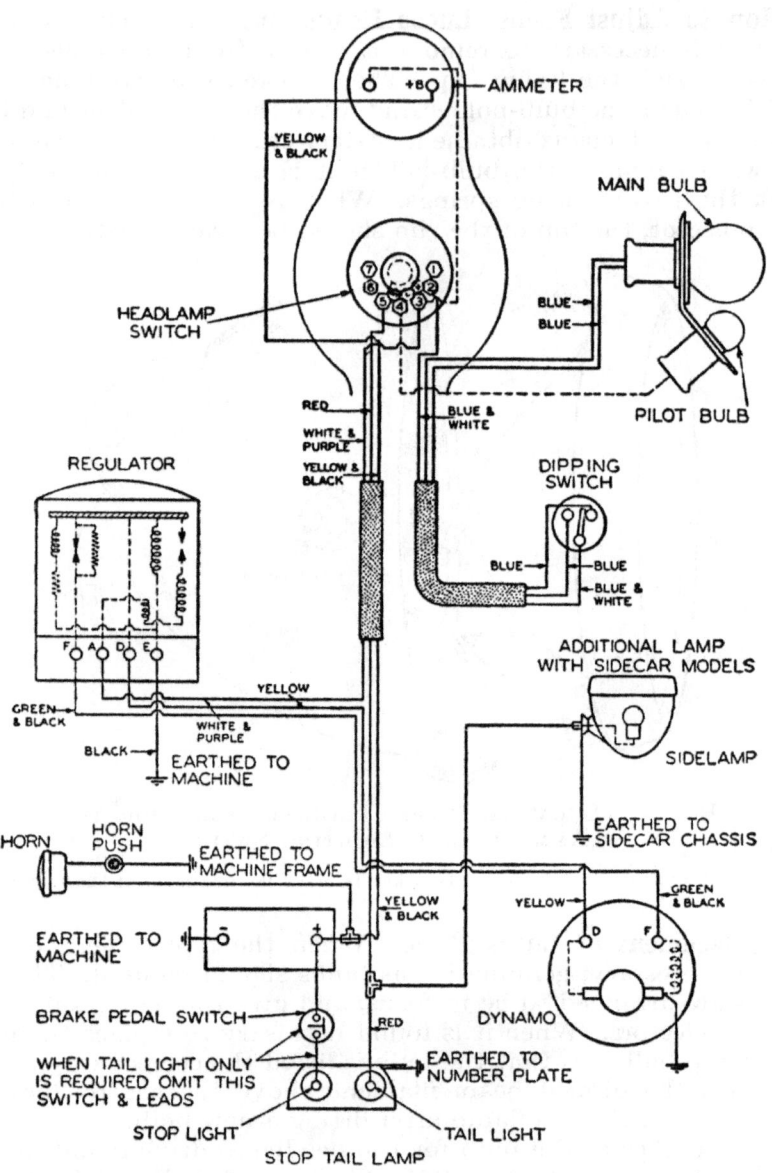

Fig. 11A. Wiring Diagram for 1937-9 New Imperials with Lucas "Magdyno," DU Headlamp, and Compensated Voltage Control

CHAPTER III

NEW IMPERIAL LUBRICATION

IN this chapter we shall consider, firstly, the lubrication of New Imperial engines and then the lubrication of the cycle parts. The author would emphasize the vital importance of correct lubrication. New Imperials are robustly built, but the moving parts are highly stressed and will perform their duty satisfactorily only if a proper oil film is constantly maintained between the contacting surfaces. In this connexion it is desirable to say a few words on the subject of running-in.

Run-in a New Engine Carefully. It is not safe to treat a new or reconditioned engine like one which has done a thousand miles or so. Such engines require to be nursed very carefully during the first 500–1000 miles, and large throttle openings must be avoided at all cost, one-quarter to one-third full throttle being all that is advisable. Do not exceed 30-35 m.p.h. in top gear, and make full use of the gearbox so as to prevent the engine overheating or labouring. After 500 miles have been covered, it is safe *gradually* to increase the throttle openings. When 1000 miles have been covered it is safe to indulge in high-speed bursts if desired.

The probable penalty for impatience in regard to running-in will be loss of engine efficiency and power output—perhaps permanent.

During the running-in period, keep a watchful eye on oil circulation. Attend also to running-in adjustments (see page 44).

Always Use High-grade Engine Oil. Four important points to remember in connexion with engine lubrication are as follows—

(1) Use a high-grade oil.
(2) Keep sufficient oil in circulation.
(3) Check oil circulation frequently.
(4) Keep the oil clean and free from dilution.

The use of an inferior engine oil is liable to beget mechanical trouble of an expensive kind. Suitable high-grade oils for New Imperial engines are: Wakefield's Castrol Grand Prix (XXL during winter); Mobiloil D (BB during winter); Triple Shell (Double Shell during winter); Price's Motorine B De Luxe (Motorine C, winter); Essolube Racer (summer and winter).

For racing on a "Grand Prix" model, replenish with Castrol R, but do not mix with a mineral base oil. See also page 43.

Engine Lubrication Systems. The lubrication systems provided on 1935-9 New Imperials may be classified in two main groups, namely, (1) the semi-dry sump system, (2) the dry sump system.

Fig. 12. 1937 Power Unit with Type A Lubrication System

The outer timing case cover has been removed, showing the internal plunger pump driven from the exhaust camshaft (see also Fig. 14).

The former type is used on most 1935-9 models and the latter type is fitted on a few 1935-6 models. These two main groups may be subdivided into three distinct systems, which for convenience shall be referred to as types A, B, C.

THE SEMI-DRY SUMP SYSTEM

This system of lubrication, in which the oil is contained within a "sump" or oil reservoir combined with the crankcase, is incorporated on all except a few models with dry sump lubrication and separate oil tanks. In common with the D.S. system, the whole of the oil is kept in constant circulation, but the engine sump is not kept "dry."

NEW IMPERIAL LUBRICATION

Lubrication System—Type A (all 1937-9 Models except Models 23, 36L). The method of oil circulation and distribution combines simplicity with efficiency. The oil contained in the large "sump" at the base of the crankcase is pressure-fed by an internal plunger pump (see Fig. 12) through ducts cast in the crankcase to the main bearings, the big-end, etc., and so out on to the flywheels. Centrifugal force throws the oil off, and it collects in the crankcase beneath the flywheels. On reaching a certain level, the flywheel rims pick up the oil and convey it to a scraper wedge cast in the flywheel housing. This scraper causes the oil to be thrown into a trough located inside the crankcase over the gearbox.

Oil from the trough is led through a cast-in oilway, fitted with a non-return valve, back into the "sump," where it passes through a substantial filter, is cooled, and again recirculated. The capacity of the oil pump is greater than is needed for efficient lubrication, and consequently three-quarters of the delivery supply is diverted by a by-pass back into the crankcase. The by-pass is situated in the web connecting the timing case to the crankcase just above, and to the rear of, the oil-filler cap. The quantity of oil by-passed can, if necessary, be adjusted by the higher of the two hexagon-headed screws, fitted with lock-nuts, adjacent to the web.

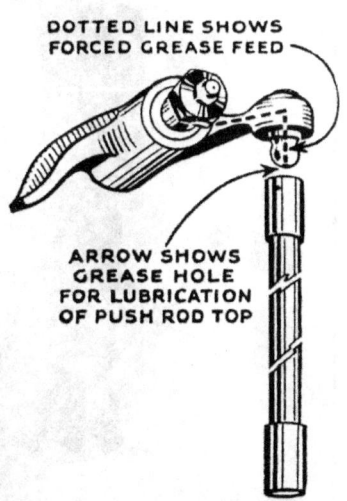

Fig. 13. O.H. ROCKER AND PUSH-ROD LUBRICATION
This applies to all engines having the Type A lubrication system.

A grease nipple is provided on the hexagonal end of each overhead rocker spindle, and grease applied here serves to lubricate not only the spindle, but also the upper end of the push-rod. As may be seen in Fig. 13, there is an oil-way drilled through each inner rocker arm and ball, which enables grease to pass into the inverted cup at the upper end of each push-rod. Automatic lubrication of the valve guides is provided for by means of a pipe leading from the oil pump to the centre of the rocker-box on the off-side. At the point where the feed enters the rocker-box, a regulator is provided which takes the form of an adjustable knurled disc on 1937 engines and a fixed hexagon-headed screw on later types. An extension of the external pipe leads to an oil indicator button on top of the petrol tank.

Lubrication System (Type A)—Maintenance. Since this lubrication system is of the constant circulation type, it is obviously

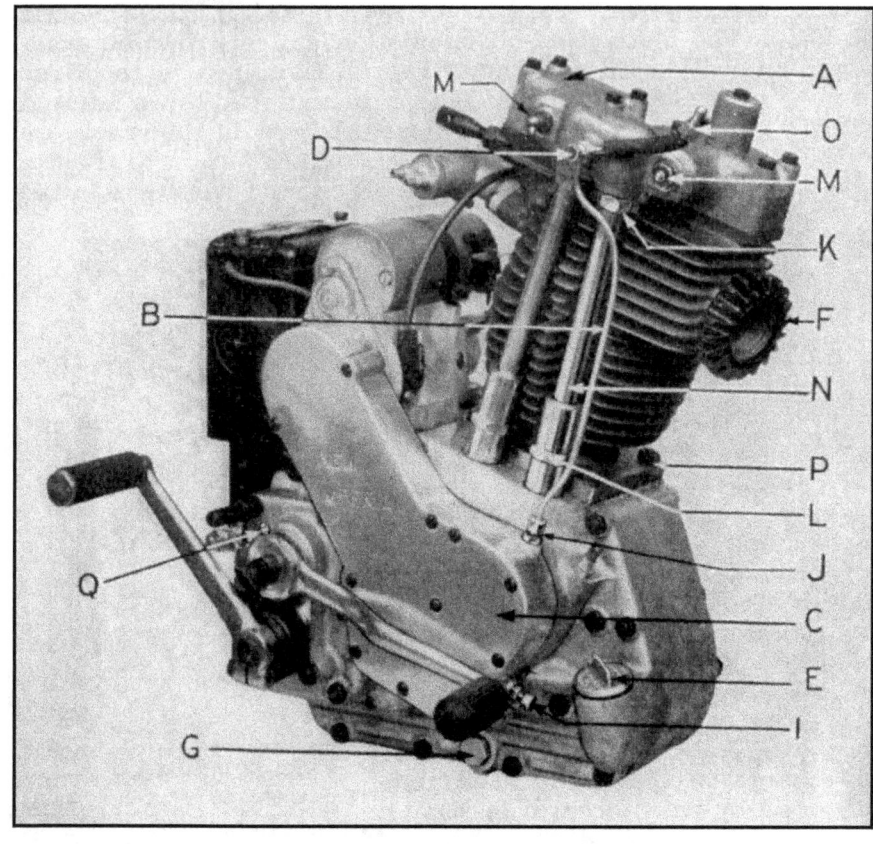

Fig. 14. 1938-9 Power Unit with Type A Lubrication System

The 1937 engine is almost identical.

A = Rocker-box
B = Oil feed pipe to valve guides
C = Outer timing case cover
D = Valve guide oil regulator
E = Oil filler cap
F = Finned exhaust port
G = Crankcase drain plug
I = By-pass adjuster screw
J = Oil pipe union
K = Upper push-rod cover nut
L = Lower push-rod cover nut
M = Grease nipples for O.H. rockers and push-rods
N = Push-rod cover tube
O = Union for indicator pipe
P = Cylinder flange nut
Q = Grease nipple for foot gear change

NEW IMPERIAL LUBRICATION

important always to keep the "sump" well filled with suitable engine oil (page 23). The filler cap E (Fig. 14) should frequently be removed (say, every 250 miles) and the oil in the "sump" topped up if necessary to within ½ in. of the top of the filler hole. Be careful not to overfill by tilting the machine. Keep a close watch on the oil indicator button situated on top of the tank. Within a few seconds of starting up, the indicator button should protrude about ⅜ in. If it fails to do so, stop the engine at once and check for an air lock as described on page 28.

About every 500 miles inject with the grease-gun some good quality H.M.P. grease into the two nipples M (Fig. 14) on the hexagon ends of the overhead rocker spindles.

It is desirable about every 1000 miles to drain the crankcase and clean the oil filter. To do this, remove the drain plug G (Fig. 14) after a run when the oil is warm, and allow the oil to flow out into a tray or other receptacle placed beneath the crankcase. To ensure thorough draining, after oil ceases to drip out, turn the engine over several times with the kick-starter, using the exhaust valve lifter. Now allow the machine to stand for a few minutes and then lean the machine over to the off-side. While the drain plug is removed, clean the filter with petrol and a soft brush. Having drained the crankcase and cleaned the filter, replenish with fresh oil as follows: First see that the drain plug is replaced and tightened up hard. Then remove the filler cap and replenish with suitable engine oil until the level reaches to the *bottom* of the filler aperture. Now replace the filler cap, start up the engine, and run it for half a minute. Stop the engine and, after allowing to stand for another half a minute, remove filler cap and top up the "sump" to within ½ in. of the filler cap. Finally, replace the same, and the engine is ready for use.

The oil pump on a new engine is adjusted to give a liberal supply of oil during the running-in period, and when this period is completed it *may* be desirable to reduce the oil supply slightly if the exhaust emits a continuous blue haze, or, in other words, "smokes." But make no attempt to adjust the oil supply unless this is *really necessary*. Except while running-in, a blue haze should not exist, though this is quite normal on accelerating suddenly from a standstill or with the gear lever in neutral.

As has already been stated (page 25), the main oil supply is adjusted by means of the lock-nut and by-pass adjuster screw I (Fig. 14). To reduce the oil supply, turn the screw *anti-clockwise*; to increase the oil supply, turn it *clockwise*. The oil supply is very sensitive to this adjustment, and the screw should only be turned *one-eighth of a turn at a time*, the condition of the exhaust being noted after making each adjustment, which on 1937 engines should be effected with the oil-feed regulator for the valve guides in the "off" position. When the correct adjustment of the by-pass screw has been obtained, the adjuster screw should be re-wired. If any difficulty in obtaining the correct pump adjustment is experienced, it is the safest policy to take the machine along to a good repair depot.

On 1938-9 engines the regulator screw D (Fig. 14) for valve guide lubrication is set and fixed by New Imperial Motors, Ltd., and this adjustment should not be altered without an exceptionally good reason. In the case of the 1937 engines, however, the finger regulator on the off-side of the rocker-box (Fig. 12) is set to the "off" position by the manufacturers and requires to be adjusted at the rider's discretion. The normal adjustment is *one-twelfth of an anti-clockwise turn* from the full "off" position. This provides adequate valve stem and valve guide lubrication, and gives a faint blue exhaust haze. By turning the regulator anti-clockwise about half a turn for a few seconds, a noticeable increase in exhaust haze occurs, and the regulator may then be gradually closed until the normal position giving correct lubrication is obtained.

If the Oil Indicator Fails to Protrude. If the oil indicator button fails to protrude within a few seconds of starting up, it is possible that an air lock may have occurred, especially if the machine has been left standing or is new. Check up in the following manner.

First ascertain that the button is not stuck by moving it round with the ball of the finger. Then start up the engine and tilt the machine over to the off-side. Should the indicator still be unresponsive, remove the union nut J at the foot of the rocker-box feed pipe B, start the engine, and note if oil issues from the nipple. If it does, allow a little to flow, replace the union nut, and watch for erection of the indicator. If no oil issues from the nipple, stop the engine and examine the level of oil in the "sump." Replenish if necessary, restart, and if still no oil issues, remove the outer timing case cover C (Fig. 14) so as to expose the oil pump. There should be some oil present in the chamber in which the pump is situated. Next remove the four screws which secure the pump (see Fig. 12); these screws are wired together. The pump itself may then be taken off, disclosing the delivery or inlet hole, which is the upper one. This hole should be primed with engine oil, and the pump refitted after carefully cleaning the ball and seat. Finally, rewire the four fixing screws, replace the outer timing case cover, and start up the engine. The indicator button should now protrude.

Should the indicator still fail to function, remove the valve retaining plug which is close to the oil drain plug G (Fig. 14), and allow the spring and $\frac{3}{16}$ in. ball to drop out. Then clean the ball and the seat on which it rests in the crankcase; also slightly extend the length of the spring. Refit the parts, and again start up and watch for the indicator button to rise. If it still refuses

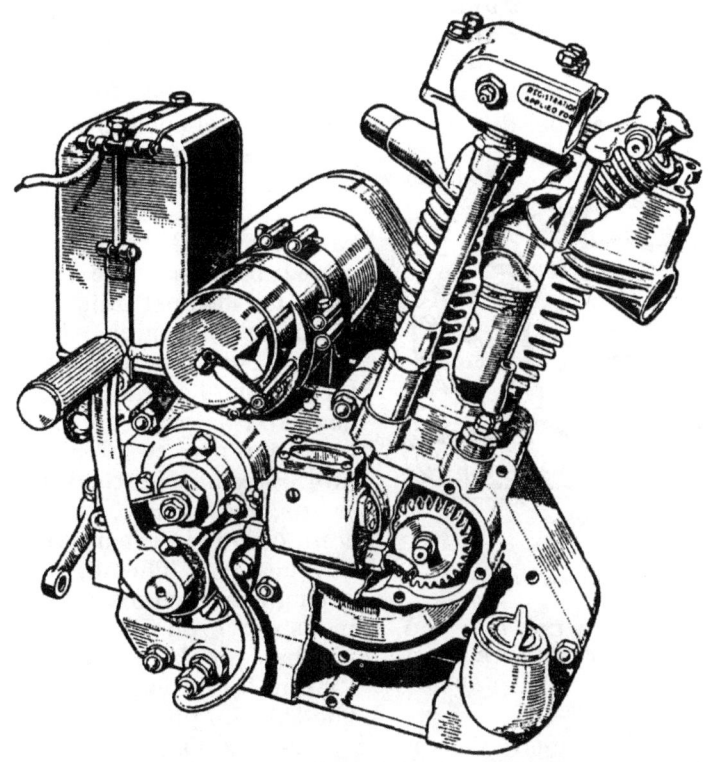

FIG. 15. 1935-9 POWER UNIT WITH TYPE B LUBRICATION SYSTEM

Observe the large "sump" beneath the crankcase proper. The arrangement of the feed and delivery pipes employed on most machines is shown in Fig. 17A, as is also the pump regulator. On the 1935-6 Models 70, 76, a duplex pump is fitted (see text).

(*By courtesy of "Motor Cycling"*)

duty, it is probable that the oil flow to the by-pass requires resetting (see page 27).

Lubrication System—Type B (all 1935-6 Unit Construction Models* and 1937-9 Models 23, 36L). This semi-dry sump system, like type A previously dealt with, is a constant circulation system, and includes an oil tank or "sump" combined with the crankcase. But here the resemblance practically ceases. An external

* By unit construction models is meant machines where the engine and gearbox form one unit, that is all except Models F10, F11, 50, 60, 90, 100.

mechanical pump is employed, and the oil in circulation lubricates *both the engine and gearbox*. The latter is a rather unusual feature.

A brief description will make clear to the reader the general method of oil circulation. Oil is supplied to the "sump" below the crankcase proper through the filler shown in Fig. 15. It is then pumped by an external camshaft-driven Pilgrim pump (which is of the duplex type on the 1935-6 Models 70, 76) through a sight-feed chamber direct to the flywheels, thence to the cylinder and piston, and forced by crankcase compression on downward piston strokes into the timing case cover, thereby automatically lubricating the cams, tappets, and tappet guides.

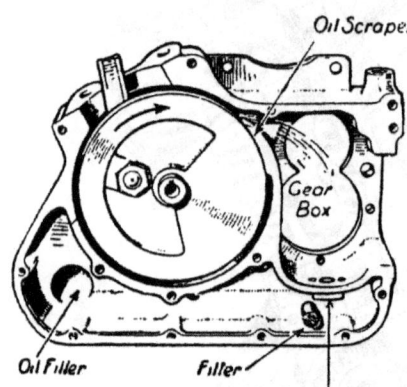

FIG. 16. SHOWING HOW OIL SERVES TO LUBRICATE BOTH THE ENGINE AND GEARBOX

Reproduced by permission of "Motor Cycling"

Surplus oil carried by the flywheel rims is deflected by a scraper in the crankcase into the gearbox, as may be understood by reference to Fig. 16, and lubricates automatically the gear trains, gear shafts, and all other components in the unit construction gearbox. The oil, after lubricating the gearbox, passes under pressure through an aperture in the base of the gearbox into the "sump," and is again forced by the Pilgrim pump into the crankcase proper for re-circulation after first passing through a gauze filter. Provision for pump adjustment, where necessary, is included, the adjustment taking the form of a screw and lock-nut on the rear side of the pump body.

In the case of the 1935-6 Models 70, 76 with a duplex pump (Fig. 17), a second adjustment is provided at the front side of the pump body for regulating the auxiliary oil supply to the push-rod upper ends, the valves, and valve springs. The pipe from the pump conveying oil to these parts terminates just above the tappet chest, the oil subsequently being conveyed to the rocker-box through a special oil-way cast through the cylinder and cylinder head fins. Oil on its way to the overhead valve gear passes through and can be observed at the sight-feed chamber nearest the cylinder. The main oil supply passes through the sight-feed chamber on the outside of the pump. Grease nipples are provided on the ends of the rocker spindles whose bushes rely on grease-gun lubrication for proper lubrication.

On all O.H.V. engines (except 1935-6 Models 70, 76) the valves,

NEW IMPERIAL LUBRICATION

valve springs, etc., are lubricated by oil mist passing up the push-rod covers. Grease nipples are fitted on the hexagon ends of the rocker spindles, and (except on the 500 c.c. Models 70, 76, and the 150 c.c. engines) there is an oil-way drilled through the rocker arm and rocker arm ball through which grease passes to lubricate the cupped upper end of each push-rod (see Fig. 13).

Lubrication System (Type B)*—Maintenance. At all times plenty of oil must be kept in the "sump," and the filler cap should be frequently removed (say, every 250 miles) and the oil in the

Fig. 17. Duplex Pump on 1935-6 Models 70, 76

"sump" topped up, if necessary, to within ½ in. of the top of the filler hole with suitable engine oil (see page 23). Keep a wary eye on the sight-feed of the Pilgrim pump, and on 1935-6 Models 70, 76 also keep an eye on the second sight-feed nearest the cylinder. In both cases the oil may be watched issuing in drops beneath the glass window.

Inject, about every 500 miles, some good quality H.M.P. grease into the two nipples on the hexagon ends of the rocker spindles. This is most important. It is desirable about every 1000 miles to drain the crankcase and replenish with fresh oil. Draining and replenishment should be effected as follows—

Remove the oil filter (see below) and then lean the machine on its side so that the oil is drained out. Now cork up the hole and pour in about a pint of paraffin. Rock the machine from side to

---

* On these machines it is advisable to place a box beneath the front wheel to ensure all oil being drained from the sump.

side and then allow the paraffin to drain out. Refill the "sump" with clean oil to the correct level after refitting the oil filter and pipe.

At least once every 1000 miles the gauze filter attached to the oil pipe union at the bottom of the crankcase (the back of the crankcase on Models 70, 76, 80) should be taken out and cleaned. To prevent waste of oil, lean the machine over on its side. To remove the filter, first unscrew the oil pipe and then the union. Clean the filter thoroughly in petrol and then replace.

With regard to oil pump adjustment, this is carefully set by

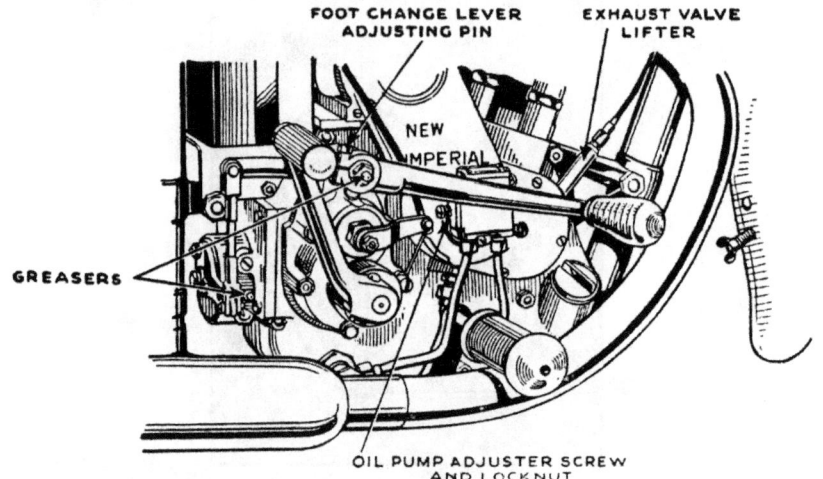

Fig. 17a. Showing Adjustment for Oil Supply on Pilgrim Pump

Various other details are also shown. On duplex pumps there is a second adjuster at the front side of the pump body.

the manufacturers, and it is rarely necessary or wise to interfere with the setting. It should be remembered that although a large supply of oil may be passed through the sight-feed chamber to the engine and gearbox, this is not wasted or likely to cause "smoking," as the oil is continually returned to the "sump" beneath the crankcase. The adjuster screw and lock-nut for the main oil supply is shown in Fig. 17a at the rear side of the pump. Should it be necessary to make an adjustment, slacken the lock-nut and turn the screw in a *clockwise* direction to reduce the supply, or in an *anti-clockwise* direction to increase the supply. Having made an adjustment, make absolutely sure that the lock-nut is securely re-tightened.

In the case of a duplex pump (as fitted to 1935-6 Models 70, 76), the secondary oil supply to the rocker-box may need readjusting, according to the conditions of usage, but it should be noted that the overhead valve gear requires only a slight quantity of oil. The feed should, therefore, be maintained at a minimum, 4 drops of oil per minute being a normal average ejection from the beak inside the sight-feed chamber.

If No Oil Passes the Sight-feed. Examine the level of oil in the "sump" and replenish if necessary. Should the oil level be found correct, remove the oil pipes and blow through them to see that there is no obstruction. Also see that the nipples are securely soldered. All union nuts must screw up dead tight to prevent leakage. Do not run the engine even for a short period with the pump out of action.

Should the sight-feed fill up persistently, this may be due to some dirt lodging between the ball valve and its seat. The remedy is to clean the ball, spring, valve seat and passages after unscrewing the glass window and removing the beak with a pair of flat-nosed pliers. Chronic filling up of the sight-feed under all conditions of temperature and oil may be due to wear of the end cam; the remedy is to fit a new part. Occasional filling up in cold weather may be due merely to the viscosity of the oil, and the remedy is to increase the oil supply for a short time, when the trouble should cure itself.

To Dismantle Pilgrim Pump. Should this be necessary (it rarely is), first remove the worm and spindle. Until this is done the plunger must not be removed, otherwise damage will result. Note that it is risky to rotate the worm with either the end plate or the end cam removed from the body of the pump. After removing the worm, remove the end plate and withdraw the plunger. On reassembly, first fit the end cam (if this has been removed) and then insert the plunger cam first, so that the two cams are in contact with each other. Then refit the return spring in the open end of the plunger and box it in with the end plate. Finally, replace the worm and spindle.

THE DRY SUMP SYSTEM

This system of lubrication, in which the oil is contained in a separate oil tank, is incorporated on the 1935 De Luxe O.H.V. models, "Grand Prix" models, and the 1936 "Clubman" models. The whole of the oil in the engine and tank is kept in constant circulation, and the engine sump is kept "dry."

Lubrication System—Type C (1935 Models F10, F11, 50, 60; 1936 Models 90, 100). The lubricating oil is contained in a separate oil tank beneath the saddle except on Models 50, 60, where a compartment of the petrol tank constitutes the oil reservoir. As in the case of the Type A lubrication system, an internal pump is used with the Type C system.

This is absolutely reliable, positive, and foolproof, ensuring greatest efficiency and economy, and consists of a double-acting plunger pump let into the crankcase just below the timing case, driven by a direct gear drive meshing with the half-time pinion. All the working parts of this pump are submerged in oil, hence wear is practically nil.

The pump, being double acting, forms two independent pumps, one at each end of the plunger. These consist of the primary pump, which pumps the oil from the tank through the pump and direct to the crankpin rollers (under pressure by way of the timing side shaft).

After oil has been forced through the crankpin bearing, it is distributed to the sides of the flywheels, thence, by centrifugal force, it is thrown to the edges of the flywheels, and then to the piston and cylinder walls. After this operation the oil drains back to the sump at the bottom of the case, and is then picked up by the return pump, which has, incidentally, a considerably larger oil output than the primary pump. This always ensures that the crankcase well is kept almost dry, and eliminates all possibility of the engine becoming flooded with oil.

The return pump forces the oil back into the oil tank where the oil return may, on removing the filler cap, be observed issuing from the pipe which projects into the tank. This provides an indication that the lubrication system is functioning properly. On Models F10, F11, 90, 100 with a separate oil tank (as distinct from a combined oil and petrol tank), a large and readily detachable filter is incorporated in the oil tank itself. On Models 50, 60 ("Grand Prix") the large filter, instead of being fitted in the tank, is situated in the base of the crankcase. This filter is also quickly detachable. A second filter is attached to the feed pipe union.

A separate supply of oil from the pump is forced to a union at the rear of the cylinder, and another pipe feeds oil to the valve guides and overhead rockers. As may be seen in Fig. 18, a regulator pin is provided just below the foot of the pipe to enable the auxiliary oil supply to be controlled if necessary. Grease nipples for the overhead rockers are not fitted. With regard to the main oil supply, no adjustment is provided or needed, the quantity of oil supplied to the big-end, cylinder, etc., being automatically correct for all engine speeds.

Lubrication System (Type C)—Maintenance. To ensure the oil in circulation being as cool and undiluted as possible, it is very important always to keep the oil tank well filled with suitable

NEW IMPERIAL LUBRICATION

engine oil (page 23). The tank filler cap should frequently be removed (about every 250 miles) and the oil topped up until the level is about 1 in. below the return pipe orifice. Under no circumstances allow the tank to become more than half empty. Before starting on a run of any length, remove the filler cap and note if the oil is being steadily ejected from the return pipe orifice. If it is, this shows that the whole of the lubrication system is functioning satisfactorily.

About every 1000 miles the oil tank should be completely drained

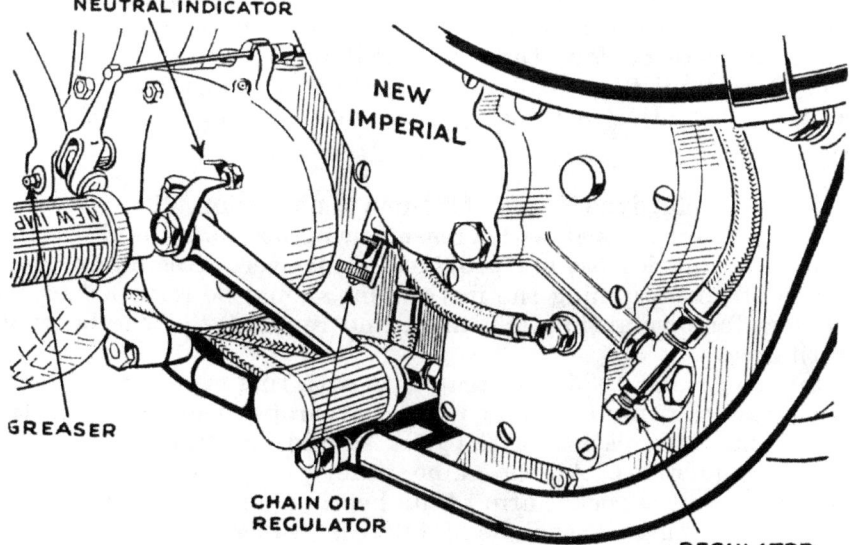

FIG. 18. 1935-6 POWER UNIT WITH TYPE C LUBRICATION SYSTEM

Showing oil regulator for valve guides, regulator for primary chain, and other details on 1935-6 engines with D.S. lubrication.

and replenished with fresh oil. Before replenishing, however, the filter must be cleaned thoroughly with petrol and a suitable brush. To remove the long filter incorporated in the flexible oil pipe union on Models F10, F11, 90, 100, place a receptacle beneath the tank to catch the oil. Then undo the union nut at the rear of the oil tank (nearest the mudguard) *anti-clockwise* and unscrew the union in the same direction. Before refitting the filter after cleaning, make sure that the union washer is sound. It is advisable to clean the filter about every 500 miles. In this case the oil need not be thrown away, but may be collected in a clean receptacle for further use.

On Models 50, 60 ("Grand Prix") the oil tank filter is attached to the feed pipe union, and the other filter is situated at the base of the crankcase on the driving side. Both filters must be thoroughly washed in clean petrol.

As has already been stated, the main oil supply is non-adjustable, but the feed to the rocker-box can be adjusted if necessary. Once the correct setting is obtained, no further attention is needed except for occasional checking. To do this, first disconnect the oil pipe from the rocker-box and, after placing the end of the flexible pipe over a tin, start up the engine and note the quantity of oil being ejected. This should be approximately 2-3 drops per minute. To increase the rate of flow, first slacken the lock-nut and then turn the regulator (see Fig. 18) *anti-clockwise*. To reduce the rate of flow, turn the regulator *clockwise*. As soon as the correct oil flow is obtained, tighten the lock-nut, recheck, and, if the adjustment is correct, refit the pipe union to the rocker-box.

Lucas " Magdyno " and Magneto Lubrication. The bearings and gears are packed with grease during assembly, and for this reason no lubricators are provided. However, after many thousands of miles running the instrument should be returned to the makers for dismantling, cleaning, and repacking of the bearings with grease.

In the case of 1935-6 instruments with ring type cam (Fig. 8), withdraw the ring cam and put a few drops of oil (thin) on the felt wick. Lubrication of the wick should be attended to about every 5000 miles. At the same time, push aside the locating spring, prise the rocker arm off its bearing, and lightly smear the bearing with grease, such as Mobilgrease No. 2.

All 1937-9 "Magdynos" have a face cam type contact-breaker (Fig. 28), and to gain access to the wick it is necessary to remove the spring arm which carries the contact and withdraw the screw to which the wick is attached. When refitting the arm, be sure that the small backing spring is correctly replaced (see page 52).

Dynamo Lubrication (Coil-ignition Models). The bearings on the Lucas type dynamo are packed with grease before leaving the manufacturers, and consequently no lubricators are provided. After a big mileage has been covered it is advisable to return the instrument to a Lucas Service depot for dismantling, cleaning, adjustment, and repacking of the bearings with grease.

With regard to the lubrication of the contact-breaker on coil ignition models, about every 1000 miles smear lightly the surface of the steel cam (Fig. 31) with some grease, such as Mobilgrease No. 2. Be careful not to overdo this. Remove every 5000 miles the split pin (where fitted) securing the spring, lift the rocker arm off its pivot, and lightly smear with grease.

Lucas "Maglita" Lubrication. In the case of the Lucas "Maglita," which is fitted to some 1935-6 models (see Fig. 9), place a spot of oil on the cam, in the holes under the contact-breaker, for the bearing, and in the lubricator at the spindle end, about every 5000 miles. No further lubrication is necessary.

Lubrication of Generator Drive. All 1935-9 models having the clutch and "Magdyno," dynamo, or "Maglita" driven by silent, helical gears (Fig. 22), enclosed in a triangular-shaped aluminium oil-bath case, do not require separate lubrication of the generator drive. All that is required is to keep the transmission oil-bath topped up with engine oil (see later paragraph). In the case of the 1935-6 Models 70, 76, 80 the "Magdyno" is gear-driven through two idler pinions off the inlet camwheel (Fig. 32A), and consequently lubrication is automatic.

On all other models the generator is driven by chain and sprockets off the inlet camwheel (Fig. 12), and the chain cover requires to be periodically removed (about every 1000 miles) and the chain greased. Work the grease well into the chain with a stiff brush. Also place a small quantity of grease at the back of the cover, just above the bottom sprocket.

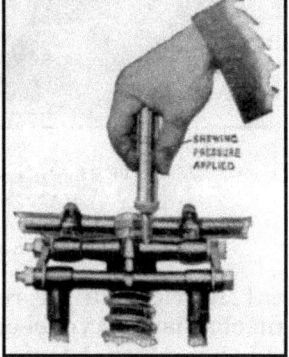

FIG. 19. HOW TO USE THE GREASE-GUN

THE CYCLE PARTS

Although lubrication of the engine is of primary importance, it never pays to neglect the cycle parts.

Suitable Greases. Suitable greases for hub lubrication and the lubrication of the various grease nipples are as follows: Mobilgrease No. 2, Shell Retinax CD, Esso Grease, Price's Belmoline C, Castrolease Medium. The correct method of using the grease-gun supplied in the tool-kit is shown in Fig. 19, where grease is shown being forced to the rear spindle of the front forks.

Gearbox Lubrication. The gearbox on all 1935-6 unit construction models and the 1937-9 unit construction Models 23, 36L is automatically lubricated from the engine (see description of Type B lubrication system on page 29), and so long as the engine is receiving sufficient lubrication, so is the gearbox also.

On all other models the gearbox is lubricated independently of the engine, and about every 1500 miles the filler plug should be removed and the gearbox topped up to the level of the filler plug* with suitable lubricant. On the 1935-6 models without unit construction (i.e. on the D.S. models), engine oil should be used; but on all the 1937-9 models without unit construction (i.e. on all except Models 23, 36L), gear oil must be used. Suitable brands and grades of gear oil are Mobiloil C, Shell Gear Oil (Heavy), Essolube 50, Price's Motorine Amber A (or B De Luxe), Castrol D.

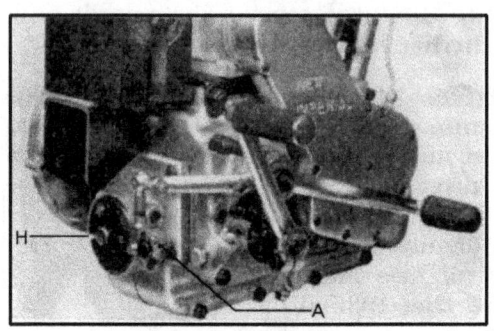

Fig. 20. Internal Type Foot-gear Change
H = Selector shaft
A = Greaser (see Fig. 45)

Lubrication of Foot-gear Control. Foot-gear change mechanism is provided on the majority of 1935-9 models, and some periodical lubrication is required. Two forms of foot-gear change mechanism have been fitted, namely, (a) the internal type, and (b) the external type. The external type is fitted only on certain 1935-6 models.

As regards lubrication of the internal type mechanism, about

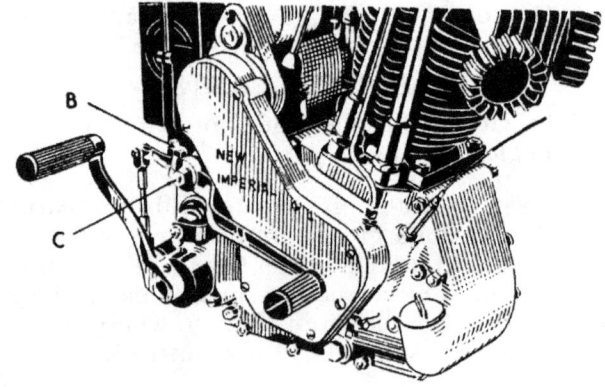

Fig. 21. Greaser for Foot-gear Change Lever
This applies to 1935-7 models except the 1936 "Clubman" models. At C is shown the greaser and at D the bolt securing the lever to its splined shaft.

every 1000 miles the grease-gun should be applied to the grease nipple A (Fig. 20) situated on the side of the foot change boss at the back of the gearbox. Also inject some grease at the same

* On 1938-9 models a separate gearbox oil-level plug is fitted.

NEW IMPERIAL LUBRICATION

time into the greaser provided for the lubrication of the actual foot-change lever. On 1935-7 models the greaser C (Fig. 21) is located in the centre of the rocking shaft, except in the case of the 1936 "Clubman" Models 90, 100, where it is situated in the centre of the kick-starter spindle (Fig. 18). On 1938-9 models with foot control, the greaser for lubrication of the actual lever is situated at Q (Fig. 14).

Where an external type foot-gear change is fitted, grease-gun lubrication is not provided, and it is necessary about every three months to grease the interior of the foot-change mechanism. To do this, remove the centre pin which holds the gear indicator in position. This has a right-hand thread and should, of course, be undone in an anti-clockwise direction. Next remove the indicator from the shaft, which is of square section. Then by grasping the foot-gear change lever, the whole of the front can be removed from the housing. Pack the mechanism (see Fig. 46A) thoroughly with grease and finally reassemble.

FIG. 22. ENCLOSED HELICAL GEAR PRIMARY TRANSMISSION

Employed on unit construction models. Note the gear drive for the generator (omitted on some models).

Lubrication of Hand-gear Control. Hand-gear control is fitted on quite a number of 1935-9 models, especially the smaller capacity models, and here again some lubrication is necessary. In order to ensure easy and sensitive gear-changing, it is desirable about once every two months (every six months during summer) to remove the gear lever completely from the petrol tank, and thoroughly clean and grease the pivot. Inspect all angle joints, pins, etc., and lubricate with oil so that they work freely.

The Primary Transmission. On all models except those with dry sump lubrication (i.e. on all except the 1935 Models F10, F11, 50, 60 and the 1936 Models 90, 100), the drive from the unit construction engine is transmitted to the gearbox by silent, helical gears running in an oil-bath chain case. Fig. 22 shows the gear transmission on a model where the electrical generator is also gear-driven. Obviously in this case (having regard to ignition timing) no engine shaft shock-absorber is fitted. On this type of oil-bath a filler plug is fitted low down towards the front of the case, and about every 500 miles the plug should be removed and the case topped up with a mixture of half engine oil and half gear oil (see pages 23, 38) to the level of the bottom thread in the filler orifice boss.

On unit construction models where the generator is chain-driven from the inlet camshaft, the upper small helical gear is omitted, the other helical gears are duplex (see Fig. 47), and an engine shaft shock-absorber is included, the whole being enclosed in an oil-bath chain case of the type shown in Fig. 23. About every 500 miles the filler plug and level plug on the side of the cover should be removed, and a mixture of engine and gear oil (50/50) poured in the filler orifice until lubricant begins to flow from the level plug hole. Lubrication of the helical gears is of vital importance, and the gears must never be allowed to run dry.

Fig. 23. Oil-bath Chain Case
Provided on unit-construction models where the generator is chain-driven.

Primary transmission on the D.S. models, referred to at the beginning of this section, is by chain, with an engine shaft shock absorber. The chain is enclosed in a metal chain case and is automatically lubricated by an oiler pipe (Fig. 53) fitted in the return oil circuit from the engine to the oil tank. A needle valve oil regulator is fitted as shown in Fig. 18, and the oil flow may be adjusted as required. To increase the supply to the chain, turn the milled disc *anti-clockwise*; to decrease the supply, turn the regulator disc *clockwise*. The correct rate of flow is 1–2 drops per minute.

Secondary Chain Lubrication. On all 1935-9 models, except 1939 Models 23, 36L (where automatic lubrication is provided), the secondary chain should be smeared with grease (e.g. Castrolease Graphited) if dry. About every 1500–2000 miles in summer and every 1000 miles in winter it is advisable to take the secondary chain off the sprockets and immerse it in a paraffin bath, allowing it to soak thoroughly so as to remove all traces of dirt. After being carefully wiped, the chain should then, before being refitted, be dipped in a mixture of warm graphite and grease, or as

Fig. 24. Lubrication Points for Spring Frame and Carrier

a poorer substitute, engine oil. If engine oil is used, the chain should be allowed to soak overnight, so that the oil can penetrate to all the link joints.

Grease Fork Spindles and Steering Head. About every 250 miles the grease-gun should be applied to the nipples provided for lubricating both the steering head (see page 80) and the fork spindles. If the former is neglected, some steering stiffness may arise and the bearings become damaged. If the latter are overlooked, nice front fork action will be unattainable. Suitable greases to use for these and all other grease-gun points are given on page 37.

Also Both Hubs. The roller-bearing hubs are tightly packed with grease on assembly, but to prevent the ingress of mud and water while riding, it is advisable to inject a small quantity of grease through the two hub greasers about every 2000 miles, or more frequently in very dirty weather. Where a sidecar is attached, do not forget the sidecar hub. Avoid injecting excessive grease owing to the danger of its getting on the brake linings and spoiling the efficiency of the brakes. Once a year the hubs should be dismantled, scrubbed in paraffin, and repacked with fresh grease.

Fig. 25. Greaser for Speedometer Gearbox

Brakes. Where a greaser is provided on the brake cam bearing, a small supply of grease should be given about every 1000 miles, but be careful not to over-grease. On some models where the brake shaft spindle passes through the frame a greaser is fitted, and it is essential that this point receives a regular supply of lubrication. Every 1000 miles, grease fulcrum pins, pedal shaft, and all brake joints.

Control Levers. It will forestall the time when the Bowden control cables snap if a certain amount of oil or grease be periodically applied at those points where they are apt to bind on the control mechanism on the handlebars. When fitting new cables and casings, the latter should be charged with grease. A piece of rubber tubing and a grease-gun will facilitate matters.

Do Not Forget the Spring Frame. On those models with a spring frame, it should be remembered that all moving parts are fitted with grease nipples. It is very important to apply the grease-gun to these nipples, shown at *G* (Fig. 24), frequently,

NEW IMPERIAL LUBRICATION

otherwise unnecessary wear will occur. Do not forget to lubricate the pivot pins of the carrier (where fitted).

Lubrication of Speedometer Drive. The speedometer gearbox is supplied with a grease nipple (Fig. 25), and a supply of grease should be forced into the gearbox once every three months. Do not over-grease, otherwise grease may get on to the brake shoes.

Every three months the spring drive should be removed from the outer rubbing casing and thoroughly greased. This is of essential importance.

New Price's Engine Oils. During 1949 Messrs. Price's Lubricants, Ltd. introduced an improved brand of engine oil known as Price's Energol. This supersedes the well-known Motorine brand.

On page 23 Price's Motorine B De Luxe and C are recommended for engine lubrication during summer and winter respectively. The corresponding grades for Energol are SAE 60 and SAE 40 respectively. When replenishing the engine "sump," use these grades, or the others referred to on page 23, if still available.

CHAPTER IV
OVERHAULING

In this chapter we shall consider all maintenance and overhauling matters other than those appertaining to the carburettor, the lighting system, and the lubrication system, which have already been fully dealt with in previous chapters. The instructions given apply to all 1935-9 models, except the 1939 Models 50, 60 (see Preface).

During the running-in period (page 23) it is very important to attend to certain adjustments and lubrication matters. These are as follows—

At the End of 150 Miles. It is advisable to—
(a) Check all nuts and bolts for tightness.
(b) Replenish the oil "sump" or tank (pages 27, 31, 34).
(c) Replenish the primary transmission oil-bath (page 39).
(d) Grease the front forks (page 41).
(e) Check tappet adjustment (page 45).
(f) Check gap at contact-breaker (page 49).
(g) Oil cables and check adjustment.
(h) Examine steering head adjustment (page 79).
(i) Check front fork adjustment (page 81).
(j) Grease secondary chain and check tension (pages 40, 93).
(k) Check brake adjustment (page 94) and grease.

At the End of 500 Miles. Repeat the attention mentioned above and also do the following—
(l) Drain and replenish "sump" or tank; clean filter (pages 27, 31, 35).
(m) Top up gearbox with lubricant (page 37).
(n) Clean plug and check gap (page 48).
(o) Dismantle and clean carburettor (page 6).
(p) Grease overhead rocker spindles (page 27).

VALVE CLEARANCES

Occasional checking of the valve clearances is extremely important and, if the clearances differ from those mentioned below, an adjustment should be made immediately. Experienced riders can judge by the exhaust note and "feel" whether attention is needed. It should be emphasized that running with incorrect

OVERHAULING

clearances, besides reducing performance and increasing noise, may result in the valve faces and seats becoming damaged.

To Adjust Valve Clearances (1935-6 S.V. Model 80). Remove the valve chest cover at the base of the cylinder by unscrewing the knurled nut *anti-clockwise*. Be careful not to damage the washer, which makes an oil-tight joint between the cover and valve chest face. Now turn the engine over slowly until both valves are fully closed and the piston is at the top of the *compression* stroke. Having done this, check both tappets for up and down play. The adjustment should be such that *with the engine hot* no up and down play exists, but the tappets are able to rotate freely.

Fig. 26 shows a Model 80 engine with the tappet spanners in position. To make an adjustment, first hold the tappet head and loosen the lock-nut below by turning the lower spanner *clockwise* Then, while preventing the tappet itself from rotating by applying a smaller spanner to the flats provided, turn the tappet head until the correct tappet clearance is obtained. Finally, lock the tappet head in position by means of the lock-nut and again check the adjustment.

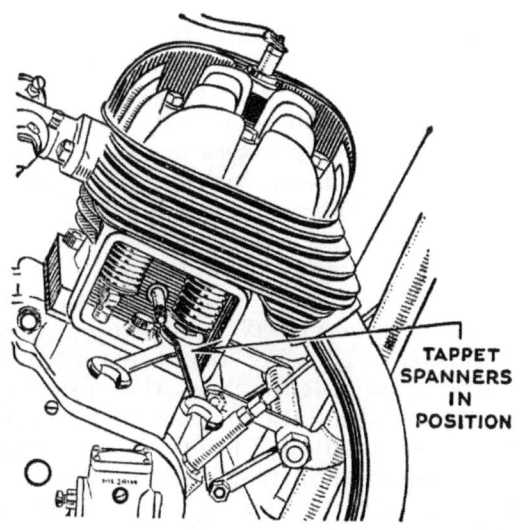

FIG. 26. TAPPET ADJUSTMENT ON SIDE-VALVE ENGINE

This applies to the 1935-6 engine with aluminium cylinder head.

Tappet Adjustment (1935-6 O.H.V. Models 70, 76). Adjustment on these engines (Fig. 17) where the push-rods pass through the cylinder is the same as for Model 80 (described above), with the exception that the adjustment must be carried out with the engine quite *cold*. The tappets, of course, must be free to revolve without any up and down play.

Tappet Adjustment (1935 Models 50, 60). The adjustment on the 1935 "Grand Prix" models is by means of adjuster screws and lock-nuts fitted on the ends of the overhead rockers. Loosen the lock-nuts and adjust the screws with the engine *cold* until it is possible to rotate the valve stem end caps without there being any up and down play. A second adjustment is provided on the tappets similar to that used on the other O.H.V. models. This second adjustment is intended to be used when the compression ratio is raised by removing the cylinder base washers.

Tappet Adjustment (all other 1935-9 O.H.V. Models). Referring to Fig. 35, first unscrew the top hexagon nuts K on the push-rod cover tubes N two or three turns clockwise. Then completely unscrew the hexagon nuts L on the bottom push-rod cover tubes anti-clockwise. Now telescope the bottom covers up the top push-rod covers so as to expose the tappets (see Fig. 34). Turn the engine over until both valves are fully closed with the piston on top of the *compression* stroke. To adjust the tappets, slacken each tappet head lock-nut clockwise. To prevent the tappet rotating during adjustment, place a spanner on the flats provided, just below the tappet head lock-nut. This applies to models where the tappets are able to revolve. Now turn the tappet head until the push-rod is able to rotate freely without any up and down movement. This adjustment must be made with the engine quite *cold*. Finally, lock the tappet head in position with the lock-nut, and again check the adjustment.

After making the necessary adjustment to both tappets, tighten the bottom halves of the push-rod covers down to their full extent, and then extend the tubes so as to screw the top halves into position. Avoid locking the top covers too tightly, otherwise the rubber joint between the two covers may be spoiled, and the rocker-box may be distorted in such a manner as to upset the tappet adjustment. When the nuts can be felt to tighten slightly, this is quite sufficient.

Exhaust Valve Lifter Adjustment. Before checking the valve clearances and at all other times, it is important to keep a little backlash (say, $\frac{1}{8}$ in.) at the exhaust valve lifter lever on the handlebars, otherwise the exhaust valve may fail to close properly. The adjustment required may be obtained by means of the cable stop, which is adjustable and situated above the front of the timing case (Fig. 17A), except on the 1935 "Grand Prix" and the 1936 "Clubman" models, where it is fitted on the off-side of the rocker-box. Loosen the lock-nut before making an adjustment and firmly retighten it afterwards.

To Remove Exhaust Valve Lifter Cable. To remove the cable on all 1935-9 S.V. and O.H.V. engines, except the 1935-6 "Clubman" and "Grand Prix" models, first rotate the engine until the exhaust valve is fully open. Then grasp the cable (see Fig. 17A)

OVERHAULING

and pull upwards sufficiently to enable the slotted sleeve on the top of the valve lifter body to be taken out. Now unscrew the body completely and slide up the cable. Withdraw the barrel nipple of the cable from the valve lifter spindle and, if the complete cable has to be removed, disconnect at the exhaust lifter lever on the handlebars also. Replace in the reverse order and be sure that the exhaust valve is fully open.

THE IGNITION SYSTEM

The Plug. A very good type of plug should always be used on both side-valve and O.H.V. engines. The reaction of an unsuitable sparking plug is a frequent cause of overheating. In an efficient engine, such as the New Imperial, great heat is generated, and a plug with a stout electrode, capable of carrying the heat necessarily imparted to it, must be used. If the tip of the electrode overheats and becomes incandescent, it tends to fire the charge

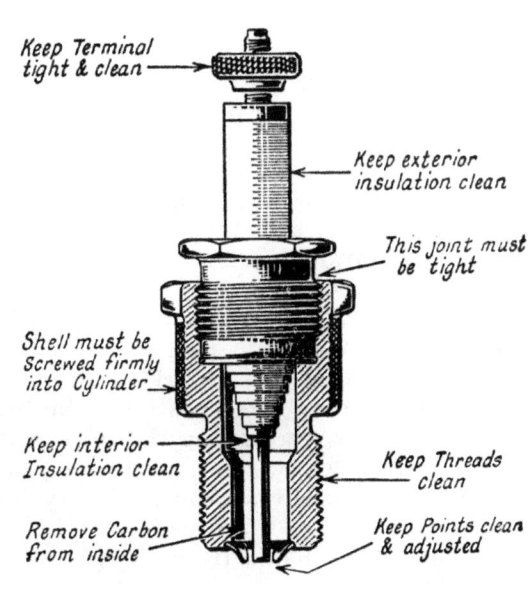

FIG. 27. PLUG MAINTENANCE AT A GLANCE

too soon, even whilst the piston is ascending on the compression stroke, resulting in a pinking noise, and imposing a severe braking action on all parts, overheating the cylinder head and piston, and very quickly causing damage to the engine as a whole. Seized engines are very often caused by unsuitable sparking plugs.

Suitable Types. Suitable plugs in the K.L.G. and Lodge range are as follows: On earlier O.H.V. engines requiring an 18 mm. plug, fit a Lodge HI or a K.L.G. M60; on O.H.V. engines where a 14 mm. plug is needed, fit a Lodge H14 or HNP. If the K.L.G. type is used, fit a K.L.G. F70. All "Grand Prix" models take 14 mm. plugs, and suitable types are the Lodge H14 and the K.L.G. F70. In the case of the 1935-6 S.V. engines (Model 80), fit a Lodge C3 or a K.L.G. M50. If not fitted, it is advisable to buy and fit a waterproof plug terminal (see page 101).

Plug Maintenance. Occasionally clean the sparking plug with petrol, and scrape the electrode points lightly with a sharp pocket knife, afterwards checking the gap between them with a feeler gauge, which should be ·018 in. to ·020 in.* with "Magdyno," "Maglita," and magneto ignition, and also with coil ignition. Always bend the outer (earth) electrode(s). The reach of the sparking plug is also of importance. The sparking plug should be frequently inspected. It is susceptible to oiling-up, especially during the running-in period and after decarbonizing or reboring.

An excellent gadget for quick plug cleaning consists of a metal reservoir containing petrol and steel wires. The plug is screwed into this and then vigorously shaken until clean. However, at considerable intervals it is wise to dismantle the plug and clean it thoroughly, which is not really possible without taking the plug to pieces. All Lodge and K.L.G. plugs are of the three-piece type, and they have Sintox or Corundite insulation respectively. These insulators were evolved through experience with aircraft plugs. A combined plug detacher and box spanner, which facilitates plug removal, inspection and cleaning, can be obtained from K.L.G. Sparking Plugs, Ltd.

To take a plug to pieces, grip the hexagon portion of the plug body in a vice, tightening the jaws just enough to hold the plug, and then unscrew the gland nut with a box spanner. Alternatively, a plug-detaching tool may be used for dismantling the plug. In the case of three-piece plugs, the insulated centre portion can be detached from the gland nut as soon as the latter is removed.

After dismantling the sparking plug, clean the plug insulation by washing with petrol or with paraffin. Afterwards remove all soot and carbon deposits, by using fairly coarse emery cloth or glass-paper. Then again wash the insulation with petrol or paraffin. After cleaning the insulation thoroughly, polish with a soft, dry rag. Clean the firing point (except on a Lodge HNP) by polishing with *fine* emery cloth, and then scrape all deposits from the earth (outer) points and inside of the plug body with a pocket-knife or wire brush, finally rinsing the body in petrol and afterwards drying it.

Before reassembling the plug, make sure that the internal washer in the plug body is seating properly, and that there is no grit between the insulator and the metal body. When reassembling, tighten the gland nut securely so as to make a gas-tight joint. Before refitting in the cylinder head, check the gap(s)

---

* With K.L.G. plugs it is recommended by the plug makers that the gap be set to ·015 in. to ·018 in. for coil and magneto ignition. A suitable plug gap setting gauge is obtainable on application to Lodge Plugs, Ltd., of Rugby, or K.L.G. Sparking Plugs, Ltd., Cricklewood Works, N.W.2.

with a feeler gauge and, if necessary, adjust. To adjust, tap the earth electrode point(s) inwards or bend outwards according to whether it is desired to decrease or increase the size of the gap(s) respectively. During the running-in period, plugs require more frequent attention than they do later on, due to the fact that oil is apt to get on the points.

Method of Testing a Plug. A quick method of testing a plug in the event of ignition trouble occurring is to remove it with the h.t. lead attached, clean and adjust it as described above if necessary, and lay it on the cylinder head with the terminal clear, and note whether it sparks satisfactorily on kicking the engine over. In daylight, sparking may be barely perceptible, but distinct clicks should be heard. If no spark occurs, remove the plug and hold the h.t. lead close to the cylinder finning while rotating the engine. If still no spark occurs, the h.t. lead must be defective, or else the trouble lies with the generator, probably the contact-breaker.

Contact-breaker Trouble. Contact-breakers are, broadly speaking, of two types: (*a*) the stationary type, where the contacts and rocker arm do not rotate; (*b*) the rotating type, where the complete contact-breaker rotates. The former type has now come into general use. In connexion with contact-breaker maintenance, it should be stated that it is not wise to make adjustments unless really necessary, though periodical cleaning and inspection of the contacts is desirable. Contact-breaker trouble may consist of (1) sluggish rocker arm action; (2) incorrect "break"; (3) pitted contacts; (4) dirty or loose contacts, and (5) incorrect timing of the "break." To avoid contact-breaker trouble, the New Imperial owner should attend to certain maintenance routine, which is described hereafter.

Care of Lucas " Magdyno " (Ignition Unit). The Lucas "Magdyno" is provided with ball bearings throughout, which are packed with grease before leaving the manufacturers. Fresh lubricant should not be required under normal circumstances before some 12,000 miles (see page 36).

The contacts of the contact-breaker should be examined on a new machine after the first 150 miles, again after 500 miles, and subsequently about every 1000 miles; and if the "break," with the contacts full open, should be considerably more or less than will just hold a 12 thou' (·012 in.) blade of a feeler gauge, they should be adjusted. Too great a gap will advance the timing. A special magneto spanner is provided, which includes a gauge for checking the "break." It is unnecessary to remove the contact-breaker to make this adjustment. All that is necessary is to revolve the engine until the contacts are wide open, slacken the lock-nut securing the fixed contact screw (Figs. 28, 29), and then adjust the screw until the correct gap is obtained.

If it becomes necessary to take a ring cam type contact-breaker (Fig. 29) off, unscrew the long taper fixing screw, and withdraw the contact-breaker bodily. The contacts only need attention at long intervals, and the reader should not interfere unnecessarily with them.

The contact points themselves must be kept scrupulously clean.

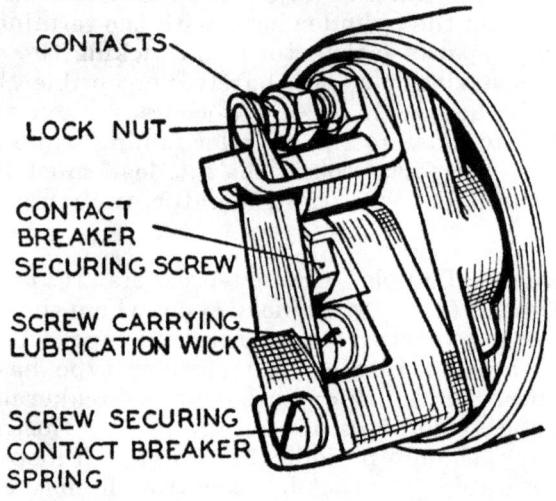

Fig. 28. The Lucas Face Cam Type Contact-breaker
1937-9 "Magdynos" have this type of contact-breaker, but on 1935-6 models a ring cam type (Figs. 8, 29) is fitted.

On examination after a big mileage the contacts may be found to have irregular and dull surfaces due to burning (especially if the contacts have not been kept clean and properly adjusted), and if such is found to be the case it is necessary to polish them up, otherwise misfiring and rapid deterioration of the contacts will inevitably follow. To polish up the contacts, use a fine carborundum stone or emery cloth (do not use a file), and with the rocker arm or spring arm removed polish the contacts until all pitting is removed and the contact surfaces are bright all over. Be careful to keep the surfaces "square" as well as uniform. To remove the rocker arm on a ring cam type contact-breaker, proceed as follows:

Withdraw the contact-breaker from its housing by unscrewing the hexagon-headed screw (Fig. 29) in the centre by means of the magneto spanner. The complete contact-breaker can then be pulled off the tapered end of the armature to which it is keyed.

Next push aside the locating spring and with the magneto spanner prise off the rocker arm from its bearings as shown on Fig. 30. After polishing the contacts, wipe away all traces of dirt and

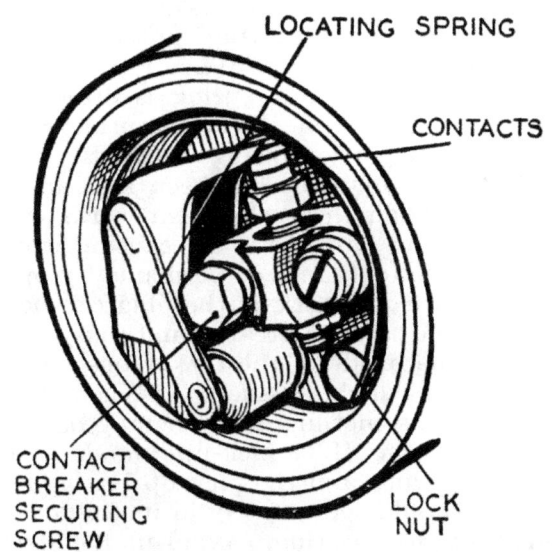

FIG. 29. THE LUCAS RING CAM TYPE CONTACT-BREAKER
Fitted on 1935-6 New Imperials with "Magdyno" ignition.

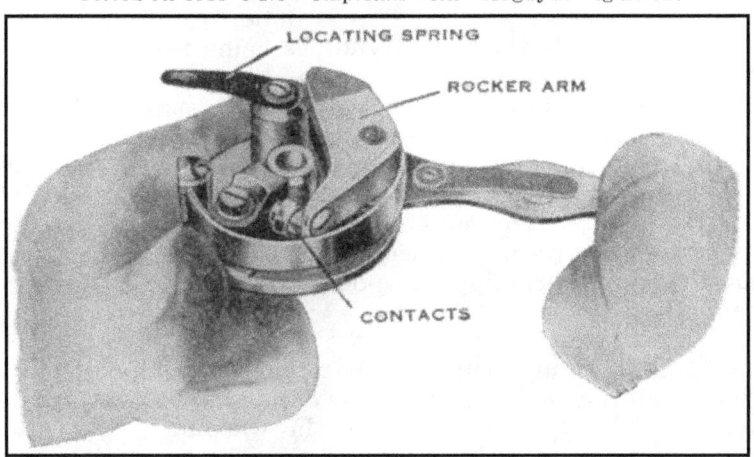

FIG. 30. HOW TO REMOVE ROCKER ARM FROM "MAGDYNO" RING CAM CONTACT-BREAKER
(*Joseph Lucas, Ltd.*)

metal dust with a rag moistened in petrol. When refitting the contact-breaker, be very careful to see that it engages the key-way on the end of the armature properly, otherwise the ignition timing may be upset. Also, when tightening the fixing screw, avoid using excessive force.

All recent Lucas "Magdynos" have a face cam type contact-breaker (Fig. 28), and in order to clean and dress the contacts, the spring arm carrying the moving contact should be removed by withdrawing the fixing screw. When replacing the arm, make certain that the small backing spring is fitted in its original position, i.e. immediately beneath the securing screw and spring washer, with the bent portion facing outwards.

Occasionally, if the machine has been kept in a damp place, the fibre bush on which the rocker arm works (ring cam type) will swell and cause the arm to stick, causing irregular firing of the engine. If the contacts remain permanently open, the engine cannot be started, for no spark at the plug can occur. The best cure is to remove the contact-breaker and rocker (see above) and rub the whole of the inside of the rocker bush with the head of a live safety match, which is usually sufficient to effect a cure. In exceptional cases, something rougher may be needed.

The moulding of the H.T. pick-up should occasionally be cleaned with a dry cloth and the pick-up brush should be examined. The brush should move freely in its holder and bed down on to the track of the slip-ring. Avoid undue stretching of the brush spring.

It will prevent misfiring and render starting easier if the slip-ring is cleaned occasionally. This is done by taking off the h.t. terminal and, while the "Magdyno" is being revolved by slowly turning the engine over, inserting a lead pencil, the end of which is covered with a clean rag moistened with petrol. The pencil should be pressed against the rotating slip-ring.

Beyond the above-mentioned points, the "Magdyno" should not be interfered with. If internal trouble develops, return the instrument to the makers for repair. Never attempt to remove the armature, because if this is done in an unskilful manner (without bridging the poles), the magnets may become demagnetized.

Coil Ignition Equipment. The equipment used on 1935-9 coil ignition models comprises the Lucas dynamo, the contact-breaker attached to the dynamo, the coil, the warning lamp, and the battery. Dynamo and battery maintenance have already been dealt with on pages 13-19 respectively. It remains to deal with the dynamo contact-breaker, the coil, and warning lamp.

The Dynamo Contact-breaker (Coil Ignition). Lubrication of the contact-breaker has already been dealt with on page 36. Occasionally the moulded cover should be removed and the

OVERHAULING

contacts (Fig. 31) examined. They must always be absolutely clean and free from grease or oil. Should the contacts on examination be found to be blackened, burned, or pitted, it will be necessary to polish them as in the case of the Lucas "Magdyno" with fine carborundum stone or emery cloth, afterwards wiping them quite clean with a rag moistened in petrol. Cleaning and polishing of the contacts is greatly facilitated by removing the rocker arm from its housing. Remove the nut and collar securing the rocker

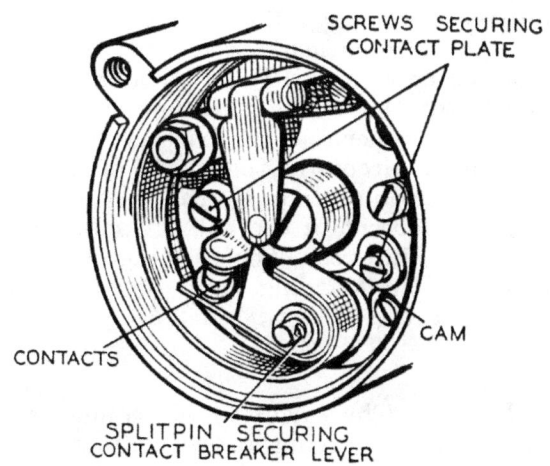

FIG. 31. LUCAS CONTACT-BREAKER (COIL IGNITION)
This contact-breaker is fitted on the end of the dynamo.

arm spring, and then lift the rocker arm off its pivot. After cleaning and polishing the contacts (both of which are fixed), refit the rocker arm, replace the collar and nut, and check the gap between the contacts.

The correct contact-breaker gap is ·008 in.–·010 in. Adjustment ordinarily is required only at long intervals, and should not be made unless really necessary. To check the gap, rotate the engine slowly until the contacts are fully opened, and then slide a feeler gauge of the correct thickness between them. To adjust the gap, slacken the two screws (one screw on 1935-6 models) securing the contact plate (Fig. 31), and adjust the position of the plate carrying the stationary contact until the correct gap is obtained. Afterwards securely retighten the screw(s) and again check the "break."

When refitting the moulded cover it is essential to make sure that the hinged steel blade on the contact-breaker makes good contact with the condenser within the cover. Arcing at the contacts (and consequent burning) will occur if the blade fails to press firmly against the case

The Coil. This requires no attention other than to see that the exterior is kept perfectly clean, especially the terminals. Both l.t. and h.t. terminals must be kept done up tight and kept free from oil or water.

The Warning Lamp. The purpose of the warning lamp incorporated with the ammeter at the back of the headlamp is to warn the driver when the ignition is switched on. As soon as the dynamo commences to charge (i.e. while the engine is running), the warning lamp automatically goes out, but it continues to glow red when the ignition is left on with the engine stationary or idling. Whenever the machine is left standing, *the ignition must be switched off*, otherwise the battery may discharge itself through the primary circuit in the event of the contacts being closed. The coil ignition system, by the way, should continue to function if there is current in the battery sufficient to cause the headlamp to burn a dull red. The running of the machine is in no way affected by the warning lamp burning out, but should this happen, replace the bulb with a 2·5 volt, 0·2 amp. bulb as soon as possible.

Condenser Trouble. The symptom of condenser trouble is a pronounced tendency for arcing at the contacts, giving rise to a complete stoppage or misfiring. If chronic burning of the contacts takes place, suspect the condenser immediately.

Care of Lucas " Maglita." For information on lubrication the reader is referred to page 37. The brush gear and commutator have also been dealt with on pages 14, 16 respectively. As regards the contact-breaker, examine the contacts (Fig. 9) occasionally and, if necessary, clean and adjust the gap between them. If the contacts are pitted, polish as in the case of the "Magdyno" with fine carborundum stone or emery cloth, afterwards cleaning with a petrol-moistened rag. The correct gap at the contacts is ·010 in. with the contacts fully opened. Adjustment may be effected by means of the adjustable contact screw and lock-nut situated on top of the cam housing. Beyond periodical attention to the contact-breaker, no further attention is required. Never try and remove the armature of the "Maglita," as this would almost certainly demagnetize it. If a thorough overhaul is called for, the best plan is to return the instrument to a Lucas Service Depot for expert attention. It should be noted that the current drawn from the "Maglita" for charging the battery and lighting the lamps has no effect on the ignition system, but a dead short in the lighting circuit may occasion misfiring.

OVERHAULING

" Magdyno " Chain Adjustment (1935-6 Models F10, F11, 50, 60, 90, 100). On these models with dry sump lubrication the adjustment of the "Magdyno" or magneto chain is effected by sliding the instrument backwards or forwards in the slots in the gearbox and engine plates (see Fig. 53). The chain is correctly tensioned when it has an up and down movement of approximately ¼ in. mid-way between the armature and inlet camshaft sprockets. The tension should be checked whenever greasing is carried out (page 37). To retension the chain, first loosen the two "Magdyno" or magneto platform bolt nuts on the near-side of the machine, and then push the instrument backwards or forwards according to whether it is desired to tighten or slacken the chain. After retensioning the chain correctly, firmly retighten both nuts.

" Magdyno " Chain Adjustment (1936 Models 36, 46). On these two "Unidyno" models the "Magdyno" is held in position by two cross-bolts. The rear bolt head is situated beneath the "Magdyno" on the off-side and the other bolt head on the near-side. In order to retension the chain so that it has a ¼ in. up and down movement mid-way between the sprockets, loosen the two bolts with a spanner in an *anti-clockwise* direction, and then slide the "Magdyno" backwards or forwards as required to obtain the correct tension. Always check the tension when re-greasing the chain (page 37). On all other 1935-6 models the generator chain is gear-driven and, of course, the question of chain tension does not arise.

" Magdyno " Chain Adjustment (all 1937-9 Models except 23, 36L). Four bolts passing through the steel "Magdyno" platform hold the "Magdyno" in position. As in the case of the other models referred to above, the chain tension should be checked whenever the chain case cover is removed for greasing of the chain (page 37). It is correct when there is an up and down movement of ¼ in. mid-way between the sprockets (Fig. 12). It is not necessary to disturb the "Magdyno" mounting in order to re-tension the chain, as this can be done by slackening the nuts on the bolts which retain the platform itself, and tipping the instrument backwards or forwards until the correct tension is obtained. Afterwards firmly retighten the nuts. In the case of Models 23, 36L the dynamo for coil ignition or the "Maglita" is driven by a helical gear off the clutch (Fig. 22).

IGNITION AND VALVE TIMING

It is necessary to retime the ignition whenever the drive to the "Magdyno," "Maglita," magneto, or dynamo is disturbed. Rarely indeed is it necessary to retime the valves, this only being necessary when the timing gears are removed. However, "just in case," the author will deal with both ignition and valve timing.

To Retime Ignition (1935-9 Models with "Maglita" or Coil Ignition). As may be seen in Fig. 32, the "Maglita" or dynamo on the 1935-6 Models 23, 23DL, 25, 27, 30, 30DL, 35, 37, 40, 45, 47, 49, and the 1937-9 Models 23, 36DL, is driven by a helical toothed brass driving pinion off the clutch. To retime the ignition, proceed as follows.

First remove the outer half of the primary transmission cover and then loosen the lock-nut (R.H. thread) which secures the driving pinion to the tapered end of the "Maglita" or dynamo armature. The pinion may now be readily removed (Fig. 32). If stiff, an extractor tool (obtainable from New Imperial stockists) must be employed. Next remove the sparking plug and turn the engine over until the piston is at top dead centre (T.D.C.) on the compression stroke* (both valves fully closed). To find the exact T.D.C. position, insert a piece of stiff wire through the hole and "rock" the engine until the position is found where no movement is imparted to the wire. Alternatively, a proprietary T.D.C. indicator may be employed. Having found T.D.C., fully retard the ignition lever and rotate the armature until the points of the contact-breaker are just commencing to "break." With the armature in this position and the piston still dead on T.D.C., refit the "Maglita" or dynamo pinion and lock tightly in position with the lock-nut. Finally, again check the ignition timing and,

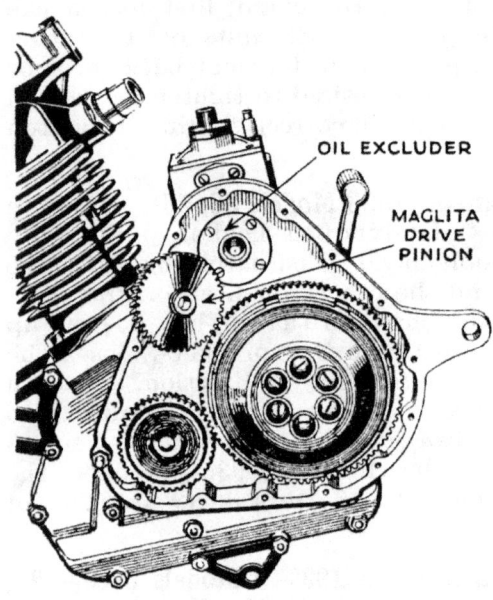

Fig. 32. Showing "Maglita" Model with Driving Pinion Removed from Armature

---

* On New Imperials the "Maglita" or dynamo (coil ignition) is driven at *engine* speed, and therefore it is of no real importance whether the piston is set at T.D.C. on the compression or exhaust stroke. This does not apply to other models.

OVERHAULING

if correct (sometimes tightening the lock-nut upsets it), replace the outer half of the primary transmission cover. Run up the engine and check performance.

To Retime Ignition (1935-6 " Magdyno " Models 70, 76, 80). On these models, as may be seen in Fig. 32A, the "Magdyno" is driven from the inlet camwheel by a train of spur gears consisting

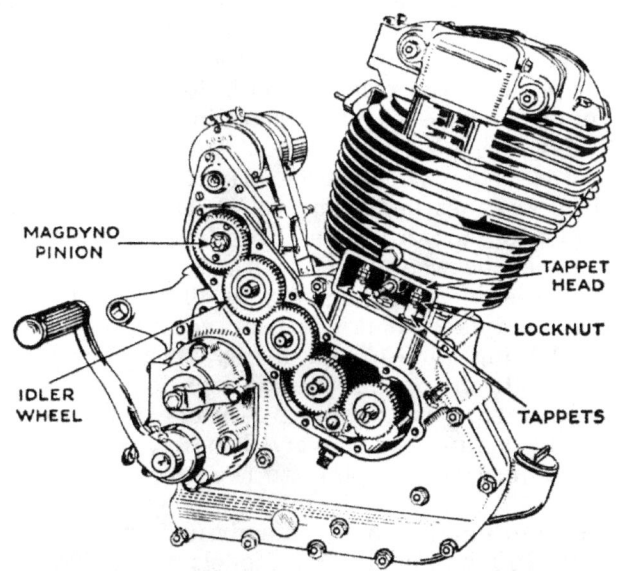

FIG. 32A. THE TIMING GEAR AND "MAGDYNO" DRIVE ON THE 1935-6 MODELS 70, 76, 80

The tappet cover is shown removed as well as the timing cover, exposing the tappet adjustment.

of the "Magdyno" pinion and two idler wheels. To retime the ignition, proceed as follows.

First of all disconnect the oil pipes from the duplex Pilgrim pump at the pump end, and then completely remove the pump from the timing case cover. The latter should now be removed. Loosen the lock-nut which secures the "Magdyno" top driving pinion to the armature shaft taper and withdraw the pinion, using, if necessary, a withdrawal tool (obtainable from New Imperial stockists). If a withdrawal tool is not at hand, and the pinion is tight on its taper, do not bother about pinion removal, but take out the idler wheel instead (see Fig. 32A). Next remove the sparking plug and gently rotate the engine until the piston is at T.D.C. on the *compression stroke*, with both valves fully closed. Insert a piece of stiff wire through the plug hole and make a nick on the wire where it touches the top of the hole, with the piston exactly at T.D.C. (see previous notes about finding T.D.C.). The wire should then be removed and a second nick or scratch made 12 mm. above it for Models 70, 76 (O.H.V.), or 10 mm. above it in the case of Model 80 (S.V.). It should be noted that 12 mm. is equivalent to just under ½ in., while 10 mm. is equivalent to just over ⅜ in.

Replace the wire through the plug hole so that it rests on the piston as before, and slowly rotate the engine *backwards* (anti-clockwise) until the upper mark is in line with the top of the plug hole. In this position the piston has obviously descended exactly 12 or 10 mm. as the case may be, according to whether the engine is of the O.H.V. or S.V. type. Then fully advance the ignition lever and rotate the "Magdyno" armature until the contact-breaker points are just beginning to "break." To find the commencement of the "break," it is a good plan to place a piece of thin tissue paper between the contacts and note the point where the paper is released on gently pulling. With the armature in this position, replace (if it has been completely removed) the "Magdyno" driving pinion and firmly retighten the lock-nut. Alternatively, slide into mesh the idler pinion, being careful not to move the armature or engine. Again check the timing and, if correct, refit the timing case cover. Finally, replace the Pilgrim pump and reconnect the oil pipes to the pump.

To Retime Ignition (1935-6 "Magdyno" Models 36, 46, F10, F11, 50, 60, 90, 100, and all 1937-9 Models except Models 23, 36L). On the whole of the above-mentioned models the "Magdyno" is driven by chain and sprockets from the inlet camshaft, the arrangement on 1937-9 models being shown in Fig. 12. To retime the ignition, proceed as follows.

Take off the "Magdyno" chain case cover, or outer timing case cover on 1937-9 models, to expose the drive (Fig. 12), and then loosen the lock-nut securing the *bottom* sprocket to the taper on the end of the inlet camshaft. The nut has a right-hand thread and may be slackened by turning anti-clockwise. Prise the sprocket off its taper by inserting two screwdrivers or other suitable tools behind it; if very stiff, use a sprocket extractor. Having loosened the sprocket, take off the sparking plug and turn the engine slowly until the piston is at T.D.C. on the compression stroke, with both valves closed. With the piston in this position, insert a piece of stiff wire through the plug hole and mark it where it touches the top of the hole. Remove the wire and on 1935-9 500 c.c. models scratch another mark 12 mm. (just under ½ in.) above the first one. In the case of the 1935 Models F10, F11, also Models 50, 60 ("Grand Prix"), when used

OVERHAULING

for racing, the mark should be scratched 14 mm. above the first one. On 1938-9 models the correct ignition timings for 250, 350 c.c. engines are 14, 13 mm. before T.D.C. respectively (full advance).

Replace the wire and rotate the engine *backwards* (anti-clockwise viewed from driving side, except when primary drive is by chain) until the second mark touches the top of the plug hole. Fully advance the ignition and rotate the "Magdyno" armature

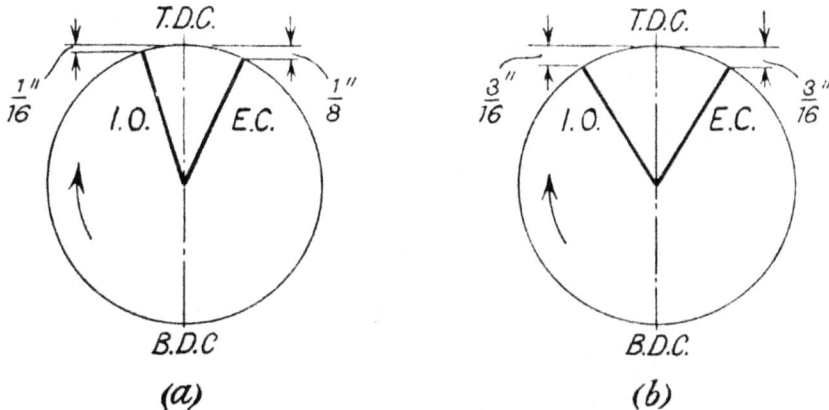

(a)   (b)

Fig. 33. Valve-timing Diagrams for 1935-9 Engines

At (a) is shown the correct valve timing for 1935-7 engines and at (b) the timing for 1938-9 engines. On 1935 "Grand Prix" models (50, 60) the inlet valve should open 28° before T.D.C. and the exhaust valve should close 30° after T.D.C. On 1936 "Clubman" models (90, 100) the inlet valve should open and the exhaust valve close $\frac{1}{8}$ in. before and $\frac{1}{8}$ in. after T.D.C. respectively. On all engines normal valve tappet clearances should be used when checking the timing.

until the contacts of the contact-breaker are beginning to "break" (see page 49), and without further moving it or the piston either, lock the camshaft sprocket nut firmly. Again check the timing and, if found correct, replace the chain case cover or outer timing case cover, as the case may be. Before doing this, check the tension of the chain (page 55) and grease if necessary (page 37).

To Retime Valves (All Models). The correct valve timing for 1935-9 New Imperial engines is shown in Fig. 33. No attempt should ever be made to experiment with different valve timings. The setting arrived at by the makers has been determined after much calculation and skilled experimental work, and is the most satisfactory.

Retiming the valves is seldom necessary, except when the

timing gear is dismantled and the camwheels removed. On all 1935 and subsequent engines a twin camwheel timing gear is employed, and to facilitate quick retiming, a dot system of marking the camwheels and small engine pinion is used. To obtain the correct valve timing, it is only necessary to mesh the inlet and exhaust camwheels with the engine pinion such that the two single dots on the pinion register with corresponding dots on the inlet and exhaust camwheels respectively. In 1938-9 engines the dots on the engine pinion should be equidistant from the top of the pinion. If in any doubt as to whether the valve timing is correct, the opening of the inlet valve and the closing of the exhaust valve should be checked. These are the points in valve timing which matter most; if correct, the closing of the inlet valve and the opening of the exhaust valve must also be right, for they are automatically determined by the contour of the cams.

To check the valve timing by the piston stroke method (as used for ignition timing), remove the timing case cover (combined with the "Magdyno" chain case on most 1937-9 engines) and proceed as follows. First make sure that the tappet clearances are correct (pages 45-46) and check the adjustment of the exhaust valve lifter (page 46). Then put the piston exactly at T.D.C. on the *exhaust* stroke, using a piece of wire inserted through the plug hole as described on page 58. To ensure that the piston "stays put," engage a gear. Now to check the opening of the inlet valve, rotate the engine gently *backwards* (anti-clockwise viewed from driving side where primary gear transmission is used, clockwise on other models) until the piston is the necessary distance before T.D.C. as shown in the valve timing diagram (Fig. 33). Use the wire method of gauging piston position (page 58), and having obtained it, mesh the inlet camwheel with the engine piston. To insert the camwheel it will be necessary to raise the tappet slightly, for if the timing is right the inlet tappet should be just lifted by the cam. The closing of the exhaust valve can be checked similarly, but in this case, after placing the piston at T.D.C., the engine must be rotated *forwards*, not backwards, in order to obtain the necessary lateness ($\frac{1}{8}$ in. or $\frac{3}{16}$ in.) after T.D.C. Always retime the inlet valve first and the exhaust valve afterwards.

As a rough guide, "rock" the engine to and fro either side of the T.D.C. position (exhaust stroke), when the inlet valve should open and the exhaust valve close in quick succession. On 1938-9 engines, as may be gathered from Fig. 33, the valve overlap is equally divided about the T.D.C. position. After checking the valve timing, replace the timing case cover, using a paper washer between the joint surfaces on 1937-9 engines.

DECARBONIZING AND VALVE GRINDING

Carbon deposits gradually accumulate on the piston and inside the cylinder head, resulting in progressive deterioration in engine performance and a tendency to knocking, which is injurious. Such symptoms indicate that decarbonizing is needed to restore efficiency. As a rule, however, it is not wise to wait till decarbonizing *has* to be done; it is better to decarbonize regularly about every 2500 miles. Thorough decarbonizing is assisted by removal of the valves, which should be ground-in. Also examine piston rings.

Items Needed. These include a jar of paraffin and some clean rags for cleaning purposes, some paper or a box on which to lay the parts, a suitable scraper such as a screwdriver, some emery cloth, a tin of metal polish, and some engine oil. If the valves are to be ground-in, a tin of coarse and fine grinding paste (such as Richford's) will be needed, also a valve spring compressor and a grinding tool for O.H.V. engines. If the engine is dirty externally, clean it thoroughly with paraffin and rags, particularly those parts about to be dismantled.

Petrol Tank Removal. The petrol tank *must* be removed prior to decarbonizing on all except the 1935-6 Models 23, 23DL, 25 27, 30, 30DL, 35, 36, 37, 40, 45, 46, 47, 49, 80 and the 1938-9 Models 23, 36L. Some riders prefer to remove the tank whether this is essential or not. Before attempting tank removal, do not forget to disconnect the petrol pipe, the oil pipe on 1935 "Grand Prix" models, and on models with an oil indicator on top of the tank, the union O (Fig. 35). On machines with hand gear control, the yoke end must also be disconnected from the gear lever. On 1935 models fitted with an instrument panel on top of the tank, it is necessary to disconnect the tail lamp, the headlamp, the positive battery, earth lead, and the dynamo leads, leaving the wiring of the panel itself undisturbed. The tank may then readily be removed. To remove the tank on all models, unscrew the four fixing bolts and lift the tank from the frame supports. Be careful not to lose the rubber insulating rubbers.

(1) **To Remove Cylinder Head (1935-6 S.V. Model 80).** On this side-valve engine the cylinder head is detachable from the cylinder barrel, and can be removed readily in order to decarbonize the piston and combustion chamber. If it is desired to decarbonize the inside of the piston and examine the rings, the cylinder barrel must also, of course, be removed (page 65). To detach the cylinder head (Fig. 26), it is only necessary to remove the sparking plug

and then unscrew the eight bolts which secure the head to the barrel. When removing the bolts be most careful to unscrew them evenly and in a diagonal order, otherwise the casting may be strained. A cylinder head gasket is fitted, and care should be taken not to damage this in any way while breaking the joint. If there are any signs of "blowing," renew the gasket. If the barrel is to be removed, detach the carburettor and exhaust pipe.

(2) **To Remove Cylinder Head (1935-6 O.H.V. Models 70, 76).** On these engines (Fig. 17) the push-rods pass through the cylinder fins. To dismantle, first remove the exhaust pipe and silencer. Then take out the sparking plug and detach the carburettor by undoing the two nuts which hold it to the cylinder head flange and withdrawing the instrument from the induction flange pins. Tie up the carburettor so that it is well out of the way. Having done this, place the piston at T.D.C., unscrew the bolts on top of the rocker-box (R.H. thread), and lift the rocker-box off. Now unscrew evenly and in a diagonal order the four cylinder head bolts and remove the cylinder head from the barrel, being careful not to damage the gasket. Place the head in a safe position and then withdraw the inlet and exhaust push-rods, being careful not to mix them up. If the piston rings are to be examined and the inside of the piston cleaned, proceed to remove the cylinder barrel (page 65).

(3) **To Remove Cylinder Head (1935-6 Models 23, 23DL, 25, 27, 30, 30DL, 35, 36, 37, 40, 45, 46, 47, 49, and the 1938-9 Models 23, 36L).** On all these unit construction engines dismantling should be carried out as follows. First remove the exhaust pipe and silencer. Then take out the sparking plug and detach the carburettor by slackening the small hexagon pin on the clip which holds the carburettor to the induction stub. With a piece of string tie up the carburettor to any convenient part of the frame. Next remove the push-rod cover tubes and push-rods. Completely unscrew the upper hexagon nuts by turning them *clockwise* with a spanner and then unscrew the large hexagon nuts on the bottom push-rod covers by turning *anti-clockwise*. Now telescope the bottom covers up the top covers so as to expose the tappets.

To remove the push-rods, rotate the engine until the piston is at T.D.C. on the compression stroke with both valves closed, and slacken the tappets down as far as possible by screwing the tappet heads and lock-nuts *clockwise*. Now ease the push-rods over the tappet heads by compressing the valve springs with a screwdriver, or using the special tool shown in Fig. 34 (obtainable from R. H. Collier & Co., Ltd.), withdraw the push-rod cover tubes together with the push-rods. The cylinder head, complete with rocker-box, may now be removed by unscrewing (*clockwise*) the four bolts which secure them to the cylinder and lifting them off. Be careful not to damage the gasket, and put the cylinder head and rocker-box safely to one side for subsequent attention. If it is desired to look at the piston, remove the cylinder barrel also as described in a later paragraph.

(4) **To Remove Cylinder Head (1935 Models F10, F11, 50, 60, and 1936 Models 90, 100).** Disconnect the exhaust pipe at the cylinder head by unscrewing anti-clockwise the finned nut with the special spanner provided in the tool-kit; leave the pipe in position. Next remove the flange fitting carburettor and tie up out of the way. Also remove the cylinder head steady clip pin and the plate. Both the pin and the rocker spindle nuts unscrew *anti-clockwise*. Take out the sparking plug and remove the external pipe leading to the rocker-box. Now remove the push-rods and their cover tubes as described in paragraph (3) on page 62. To detach the cylinder head complete with rocker-box, it is then only necessary on Models 50, 60, 90, 100 to unscrew the four long bolts which secure the cylinder head and barrel to the crankcase. On Models F10, F11 the cylinder head bolts do not extend to the crankcase. Be careful with the gasket (F10, F11) or metal-to-metal joint (see page 72). Cylinder removal is dealt with on page 65.

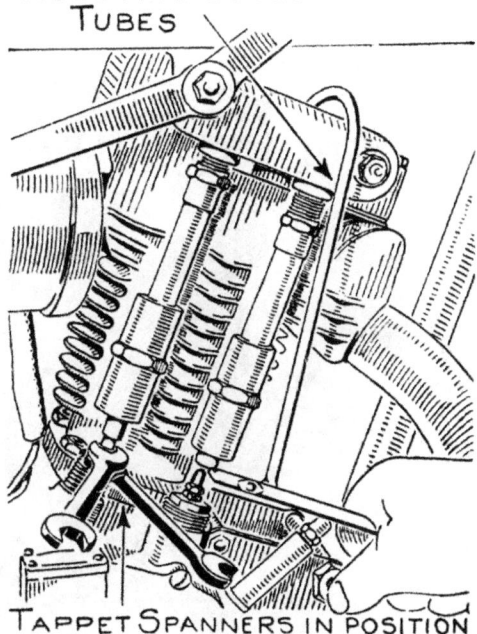

Fig. 34. Removing Push-rods and Cover Tubes with Special Tool

(5) **To Remove Cylinder Head (All 1937-9 Models except 23, 36L).** Cylinder head removal on the 25 models with semi-dry sump lubrication and internal oil pumps should be carried out in the following manner. First remove the exhaust pipe(s) and

carburettor which has a flange fixing. Tie up the carburettor out of the way and also remove the sparking plug. Referring to Fig. 35, remove the push-rod cover tubes *N* and also the push-rods as described in paragraph (3) on page 62. Then disconnect the

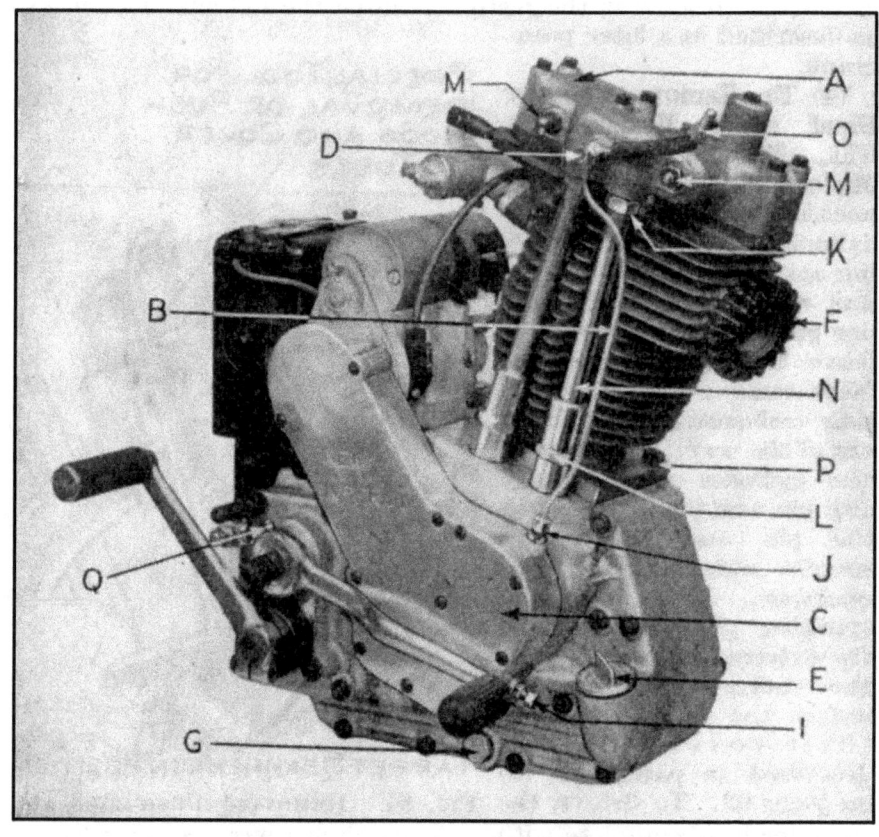

Fig. 35. 1938-9 O.H.V. Engine

All 1938-9 engines except those on Models 23, 36L are of similar design. On page 26 a key to the lettering is included.

oil pipe *B* leading to the rocker-box and oil indicator by unscrewing the nipple nuts *J* and *O*. Also unscrew and remove the eight rocker-box bolts (R.H. threads). The rocker-box, together with the oil pipe *B*, can then be removed from the cylinder head. To remove the latter, unscrew the four retaining bolts and also the engine anchor bolt, which is the rear one. When lifting the head off the barrel take care with the gasket and, if damaged, renew it.

OVERHAULING

Removing the Cylinder Barrel. Having removed the cylinder head according to the appropriate instructions given in paragraphs (1) to (5), proceed to remove the cylinder barrel in order to expose the piston. This may be done as follows.

Rotate the engine slowly until the piston is at B.D.C. with both tappets right down. Then unscrew evenly and in a diagonal order the cylinder barrel flange nuts from the crankcase studs. On the 1935-6 Model 80 S.V. and 70, 76, O.H.V. engines an additional nut will be found inside the valve chest between the tappets, and this must also be removed. Before undoing the nuts on Models 70, 76 do not forget to disconnect the oil feed pipe to the off-side of the cylinder. On 1935-6 engines with full dry sump lubrication, after removing the cylinder head as described in paragraph (4) on page 63, disconnect the oil feed pipe to the rear of the cylinder. On these engines the four long bolts securing the cylinder head and barrel to the crankcase will have already been removed during the removal of the head.

Now gently slide the cylinder barrel off the piston, inclining it towards the front angle of the frame where there is most room. While removing the barrel, grip it firmly with both hands and be most careful not to impose any side strain on the piston or connecting-rod. As soon as the piston emerges from the cylinder mouth, hold the piston so as to prevent it falling sharply against the connecting-rod or crankcase, either of which is liable to distort the skirt. Also cover up at once the crankcase hole to prevent dirt or foreign bodies entering. It is also advisable to stuff a rag into the top of the cylinder, whose bore is highly polished and must on no account be scratched. Examine the cylinder base washer; if damaged, renew it.

Piston Removal. Aluminium alloy pistons are fitted to all New Imperial engines, and these have two compression rings and a slotted scraper ring, except on some of the smaller engines, where the slotted scraper ring is omitted. The piston is attached to the connecting-rod by means of a fully floating gudgeon-pin, which is prevented from moving endwise in the piston bosses by means of spring circlips of orthodox type. To remove the piston it is necessary to remove the circlips by squeezing the ends together with a pair of round-nosed pliers, or by forcing them out from their slots with a scriber or other suitable implement. The gudgeon-pin should then be pushed out with the finger or with a pencil from the *driving side* towards the timing side. It is always best to scrap the old circlips when decarbonizing and to fit new ones, because should a circlip lose its springiness and come adrift with the engine running, havoc may be caused inside the cylinder. As soon as the gudgeon-pin is removed, the piston may be lifted off the small-end of the connecting-rod. A nick should be made on one end of the gudgeon-pin to ensure its being replaced exactly as removed. The piston should also be marked *on the inside* for a similar reason. With a file, mark the gudgeon-pin boss. Correct piston replacement is vital, because the piston laps out the cylinder bore in a certain manner depending on thrust, lubrication, and other factors.

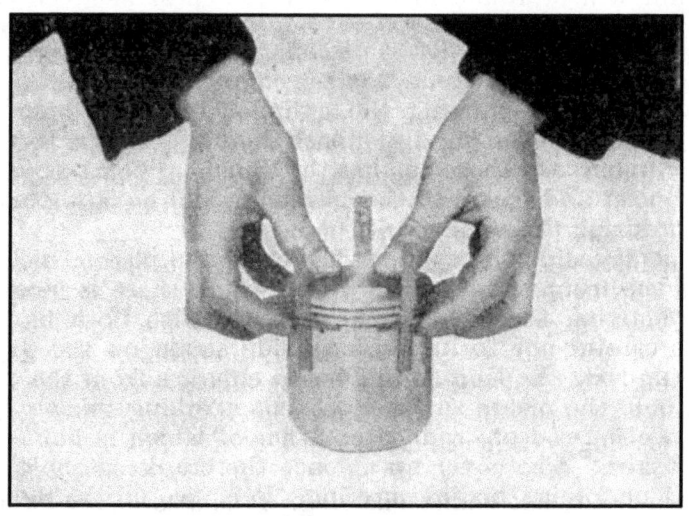

Fig. 36. The Safest Method of Removing Piston Rings

Examining and Removing Piston Rings. The two compression rings are the main-guard of the compression. They must, therefore, be full of spring, free in their grooves, and set with their slots opposite to each other (i.e. at 180°, as explained on page 74). If all rings are bright all the way round, they are obviously being polished against the cylinder walls, and are perfect, and should be left alone. If, on the other hand, they are dull or stained at some points, they are not in proper contact with the walls of the cylinder. Perhaps they are stuck in their grooves with burnt oil, and will function properly if the grooves are cleaned with a *flat-pointed* instrument.* If vertically loose in their grooves or very badly marked, the rings must be renewed.

Piston rings are of cast-iron and, being of very small section,

---

* A good scraper for decarbonizing ring grooves can be made by mounting a piece of a ring in a handle and grinding the end to a vee. Various proprietary scrapers are available.

must be handled very, very carefully. If not, they will certainly be broken. They cannot safely be opened out wider than will allow them to slip over the crown of the piston. Therefore, to put them on or remove them requires the insertion of small strips of tin, about ⅜ in. wide by 2 in. long, which are placed in the manner illustrated by Fig. 36. Be most careful to note the order

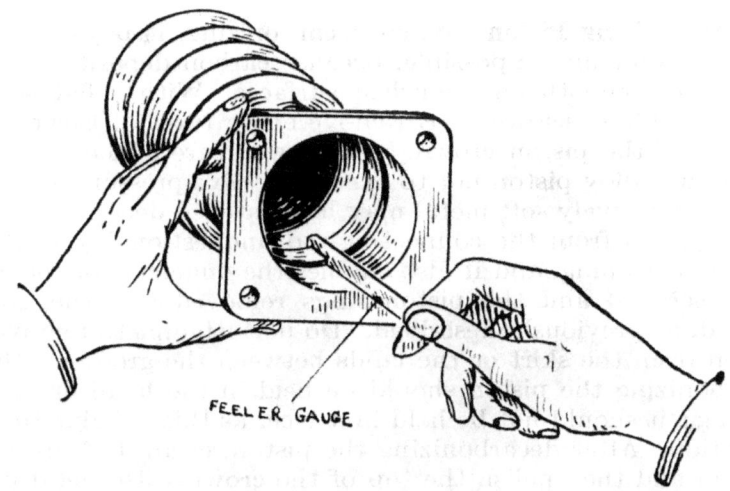

FIG. 37. HOW TO MEASURE THE PISTON RING GAP

in which the rings are removed so as to ensure proper replacement. When refitting piston rings, thoroughly clean the grooves into which they fit, and also the backs and ends of the rings. Clean thoroughly with paraffin and put a few drops of oil in the grooves before refitting the rings. Paraffin usually loosens stuck piston rings. Piston rings are made to very accurate dimensions, and it is very bad practice to attempt to "fit" oversize or undersize rings unless you know exactly what you are doing. Lapping-in oversize piston rings is a skilful job, and unless the slot sizes are exactly right, the rings will not function well, and may even produce an engine "seizure." Therefore, always use piston rings supplied by R. H. Collier & Co., Ltd. The piston rings gradually wear as well as the cylinder and the size of the gap between the ends of the rings increases. When the gap exceeds ·025 in., it is time to fit new rings. The gap in the case of new rings may be too small, and should be checked as described below. The remedy for too small a gap is to file the ends with a smooth-cut file until the correct gap (·005 in.) is obtained. For racing on a "Grand Prix" model, use a gap of ·025 in.

The word "gap" does not apply to the distance between the ends of the ring with the cylinder removed; it means the actual gap in working conditions. The only way to test this gap is to push the ring itself into the cylinder bore, making sure that it is square with the walls. To ensure this it is perhaps best to push up the piston ring with the aid of the piston. The gap may then be measured with a ·005 in. feeler gauge, as shown in Fig. 37.

Decarbonizing Piston. When decarbonizing, it pays to do the job as thoroughly as possible, because carbon deposits form less quickly on smooth and polished surfaces. With a flat scraper, such as a blunt screwdriver, remove every trace of carbon from the top of the piston crown, taking great care in the case of the aluminium alloy piston not to exert excessive pressure, otherwise the comparatively soft metal may be scratched deeply. Removal of the piston from the connecting-rod unquestionably facilitates thorough cleaning, and it also enables the underside of the crown to be scraped and the piston rings removed and the grooves cleaned, as previously described. Do not attempt to remove any carbon from the skirt or the lands between the grooves. During decarbonizing the piston should be held in the hand or in clean soft rag; it should not be held in a vice, as this is liable to cause distortion. After decarbonizing the piston, clean it all over with paraffin and then polish the top of the crown with metal polish. Finally remove every trace of abrasive by wiping with a rag dampened in paraffin.

Decarbonizing Cylinder Head. Where the rocker-box has not been taken off prior to removing the cylinder head, this should now be detached, except in the case of the 1935-6 engines with D.S. lubrication (page 63), by unscrewing the eight hexagon headed bolts which secure the rocker-box to the cylinder head. Leave the overhead rockers, etc., in position. Thorough decarbonizing in the neighbourhood of the ports is undoubtedly assisted by removal of the valves (see page 70), and this is necessary as the valves require to be ground-in.

To decarbonize the combustion chamber, turn the cylinder head upside down and then scrape off all carbon deposits with a blunt screwdriver or other scraper. The job is greatly facilitated if the head is held securely, and a good method of doing this is to screw an old sparking plug into the head and grip this with a vice. An even better method is to obtain a piece of hexagon steel bar about 5 in. long, and get one end turned and threaded to fit the sparking plug hole. The bar can then be placed upright between the vice jaws, as shown in Fig. 38.

Avoid deeply scratching the surface of the combustion chamber.

OVERHAULING

Clean up the inlet and exhaust ports with a suitable scraper (special bent scrapers are available), and do not overlook the sparking plug hole where carbon often accumulates, also the valve heads. On many engines, carbon forms on the slight ridge inside the cylinder barrel at the top of the piston stroke. Remove such deposits with great care. After scraping off all carbon from the combustion chamber, wipe the surfaces with a rag damped in paraffin. Carbon forms less readily on a smooth surface, and

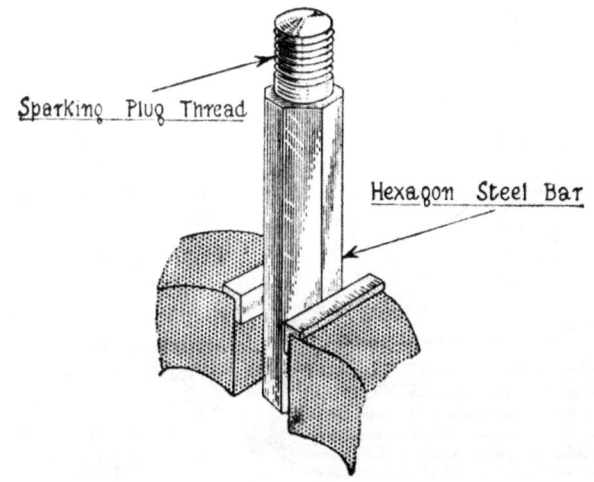

FIG. 38. A USEFUL GADGET FOR HOLDING THE CYLINDER HEAD WHILE DECARBONIZING

it is therefore a good plan to polish the combustion chamber with emery cloth, but if this is done the valves should be removed and all traces of abrasive must afterwards be eradicated. In the case of the 1935-6 models with D.S. lubrication, be extremely careful not to scratch the ground face of the cylinder head, otherwise the head will have to be ground on to the barrel.

To Remove Valves (1935-6 S.V.). The valves on Model 80 should be removed by laying the cylinder face downwards, as shown in Fig. 39, and compressing each valve spring with the special valve spring compressor illustrated (obtainable from New Imperial stockists) until the two halves of the split collet can be removed from the recess in the valve stem. As soon as the split collets are detached, the valves can be withdrawn together with the valve springs and spring caps. Be careful after removal not to interchange the inlet and exhaust valves, as they are ground individually on to their respective seats. If in any doubt as to which is which, scratch a mark on one of the valve heads. Usually, however, the exhaust valve is slightly more discoloured than the inlet valve and can thus be identified.

To Remove Valves (all O.H.V. Engines). In the case of the 1935-6 engines with dry sump lubrication (F10, F11, 50, 60, 90, 100), before attempting to remove the valves the lid of the rocker-box must be unclipped and the rockers removed. On other engines it is presumed that the complete rocker-box has been taken off prior to decarbonizing the cylinder head (page 64).

To remove the valves, first take off both valve stem end caps, and then with a suitable valve spring compressor (obtainable from R. H. Collier & Co., Ltd.) compress the valve springs until the split collets can be removed from the valve stems and the valves, springs and spring caps withdrawn. Four types of spring compressors are available for 1935-9 engines, according to type. The compressor suitable for

Fig. 39. Valve Spring Compressor for 1935-6 S.V. Engines

The tool is shown being used to extract the valves from the Model 80 cylinder.

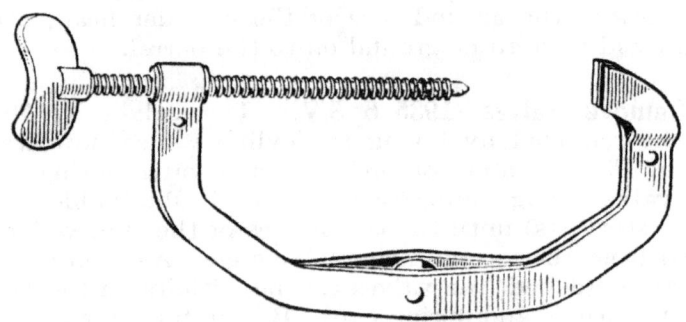

Fig. 40. Valve Spring Compressor for 1935-6 O.H.V. Engines with D.S. Lubrication

OVERHAULING

the above-mentioned 1935-6 models with D.S. lubrication is shown in Fig. 40. To use this tool (a Terry), the compressor is placed with the forked end resting on the valve spring cap and the screw in the centre of the valve head. The screw is then tightened with the wing nut until the valve spring is compressed. The valve spring compressor suitable for 1935-9 models with external mechanical pumps (such as 1935-6 Models 23, 36, 40, 70, 76, 30, and 1937-9 Models 23, 36L) is shown in actual use in Fig. 41, where its method of operation is self-explanatory. A heavier model is available for use on the larger 1937-9 models with internal pumps (such as Models 76, 36, 46, 90, 100, 110). As in the case of side-valve engines, it is very important not to interchange the valves, and if the exhaust valve cannot be recognized by its discoloration, it should be marked. It is advisable also on all engines not to interchange the split collets and valve spring caps.

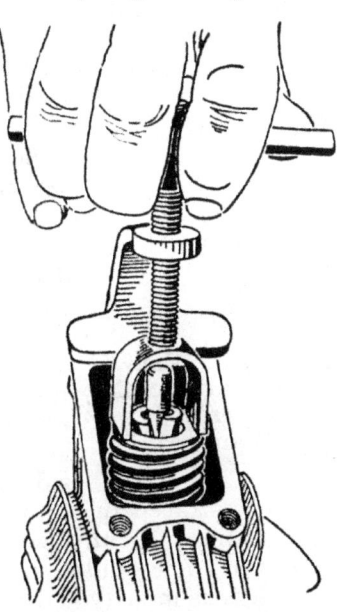

FIG. 41. SHOWING METHOD OF USING VALVE SPRING COMPRESSOR FOR O.H.V. ENGINES

This tool is designed for valve removal on engines with external mechanical pumps. A slightly different type is available for machines with internal pumps.

Grinding-in the Valves. If examination of the valve faces discloses that pitting has occurred, it will be necessary to grind-in the valves, which is a simple operation, but requires some patience. On 1935-6 side-valve engines the valve heads are slotted to enable the valves to be pressed down and simultaneously rotated on their seats with a screwdriver, but on 1935-9 overhead-valve engines no slots are provided, and the valves have to be pulled up against their seats and simultaneously rotated by means of the small valve-grinding tool illustrated in Fig. 42. This tool is obtainable from R. H. Collier & Co., Ltd., and will hold $\frac{5}{16}$ in. or $\frac{11}{32}$ in. valve stems. Before commencing to grind-in, remove all carbon from the valves and clean them and their seats thoroughly.

Only grind in valves when necessary, using a ready-made compound such as Richford's grinding paste. Do not apply the paste like jam on bread and butter, but with a rag apply just a *thin* film around the bevelled edge of the valve head. Also do not, after inserting the valve in its guide, revolve the valve round and round with the valve-grinding tool, but rotate it about a third of a turn in one direction and then an equal amount in the opposite direction. About every half-dozen oscillations lift the valve off its seat, rotate it about a quarter of a revolution and continue grinding-in, which should be proceeded with until no "cut" can be felt, when further grinding paste should be applied, and the valve face and seating cleaned and examined. Lifting the valve on S.V. engines is facilitated by inserting a coil spring under the head. Continue grinding-in until both the valve face and the cylinder head seating come up bright and the valve commences to "sing." Perfect ring contact is not good enough, and there should be some depth of contacting area. Extreme care must be taken after grinding-in to remove *all* traces of grinding paste. The valve stems may be cleaned up with very fine or, better still, worn emery paper. Do not be in too much of a hurry. The use of fine grade grinding paste is preferable and gives much better results than using a coarse grade, although if pitting is deep and extensive the use of the latter may be necessitated first. Care should be taken not to damage the valve stems in any way, otherwise the valves may not move freely in their guides.

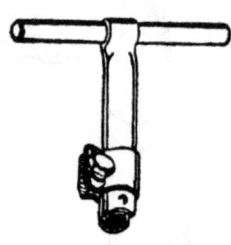

FIG. 42. VALVE GRINDING TOOL FOR O.H.V. ENGINES

The reason why valves should not be ground-in unnecessarily is because this tends to make them sink or become "pocketed" in their seats, with the result that resistance is offered to the smooth passage of the ingoing and outgoing gases. It is quite sufficient to remove all pitting from the valves and seats, but should the valves and their seats happen to be very deeply pitted (which a reasonable amount of valve grinding will not remove), the proper procedure is to return the cylinder head and valves to the makers in order to have the valve faces and seats recut. Before reassembling the valves, test them for fit in the valve guides. If the inlet valve is a loose fit, a new valve guide should be fitted, but this is only necessary after a big mileage. A worn inlet valve guide upsets carburation and causes difficult starting, blow-back through the carburettor, and loss of power.

Grinding Cylinder Head on to Barrel. A metal-to-metal joint is employed on the 1935 "Grand Prix" and the 1936 "Clubman" models (50, 60, 90, 100), and if the joint faces are discoloured, which indicates "blowing," the cylinder barrel should be fixed lightly in a vice and the face of the cylinder head ground on to the barrel face with some grinding paste. Rotate the head as if

OVERHAULING

grinding-in a valve until both contacting faces are perfectly clean. After grinding is completed, remove every trace of grinding paste and wipe the surfaces with a clean rag moistened with some paraffin. Where a cylinder head gasket is fitted (as on other engines), grinding is, of course, never needed.

Renewing Valve Springs. It is not necessary to fit new valve springs every time the engine is decarbonized or the valves ground-in. Due to their robust design, the valve springs are quite capable of service in the neighbourhood of 10,000 miles. It should be understood, however, that if a spring shows signs of undue closing and consequent weakening, it should be replaced immediately.

Reassembling Valves. After grinding-in the valves you should reassemble them in the cylinder head. Smear the valve stems with oil and replace them in their guides. Then refit the valve springs and collars, being careful not to mix up the upper and lower collars. Next compress each valve spring with the valve spring compressor and refit the split collet, making certain that it beds down properly. The application of a little grease to the lower part of the valve stem facilitates reassembly, as this enables the split collet to stick on the valve stem while compressing the springs. Finally, do not forget to replace the hardened valve stem end caps and, if these are seriously worn, renew, otherwise side thrust will be imposed by the rockers on the valves and the guides will wear. After replacing the valve stem end caps, be careful not to turn the cylinder head (O.H.V.) upside down or the caps may fall off.

After the Valves are Reassembled. It is an excellent plan to test the seats by pouring some petrol into the ports and watching for leakage past the valves. Not the slightest sign of moisture should creep past the valves until after a considerable time has elapsed. If some petrol quickly gets past the valves it is sure proof that the valves have not been sufficiently ground-in, and the remedy is (horrible thought!) remove and continue grinding-in.

Cleaning Cylinder Finning. Rain and heat quickly cause the cylinder fins of an air-cooled engine to become rusty. This does not appreciably affect the running, but it becomes an eyesore, and to a small extent reduces heat radiation. To remedy this, clean the cylinder fins with a stiff brush soaked in paraffin and afterwards paint the fins with cylinder black, which can be obtained at any accessory dealer.

Refitting Piston and Cylinder Barrel. This should be done in the reverse order of dismantling. Smear both the piston and inside of the cylinder barrel with engine oil and refit the piston the correct way round (page 66) on the connecting-rod, pushing the gudgeon-pin, which should also be oiled, home from the timing side towards the driving side. Fit a pair of new circlips and see that they bed down properly in the piston boss grooves and are fully expanded. Remember that if a circlip "goes west" with the engine running, you may have to put your hand in your pocket for a new piston and cylinder barrel. Then examine the cylinder base washer. If this is in any way damaged or cut, replace it. Also see that the cylinder barrel spigot, washer, and mouth of the crankcase are scrupulously clean.

To replace the barrel, put the piston near B.D.C. and space the rings so that the gap of the top compression ring faces to the rear of the cylinder, the gap of the second compression ring to the front of the cylinder, and the gap of the third scraper ring (where fitted) to the rear. Hold the cylinder barrel over the piston with one hand and offer the piston up to it with the other, squeezing the rings (without upsetting the position of the gaps) together until the complete piston enters the cylinder barrel. Avoid putting any side strain on either the piston or connecting rod. After seeing that the spigot beds down on the crankcase squarely and closely, tighten up the four cylinder flange nuts finger-tight first and then securely with a spanner in a diagonal order. Even tightening is important, otherwise there is some risk of distorting the cylinder flange and preventing its bedding down properly on the crankcase. Do not forget that on the 1935-6 Models 80, 70, 76 there is an additional nut to be refitted inside the valve chest, also that on the two last-mentioned machines the oil pipe must be reconnected to the off-side of the cylinder barrel. On the 1935-6 Models 50, 60, 90, 100 the cylinder barrel cannot be secured to the crankcase or the oil pipe reconnected to the back of the cylinder until the cylinder head and rocker-box have been refitted, when it is possible to tighten the whole of the assembly down by means of the four long bolts which extend to the crankcase.

No jointing compound should be used at the base of the cylinder, but the washer, if replaced by a new one, should be oiled first. Cover up the top of the cylinder barrel with a clean rag until the cylinder head is ready to be refitted.

Before Refitting Rocker-box. The rocker-box should be washed out thoroughly with paraffin, dried, and the rockers greased (see page 27). After washing out with paraffin, test the rockers for play as well as end movement. If much play exists, the rockers

OVERHAULING

should be removed and rebushed by a competent mechanic. End movement, however, can be readily taken up by means of fitting one or two steel shim washers, which are obtainable from New Imperial stockists. Four of these shims are included in standard decarbonizing kits. To remove each rocker, withdraw the split pin from the rocker spindle and unscrew the castle nut. Then turn the rocker-box over and unscrew the rocker spindle, and take it out. Now remove the large distance piece inside the rocker-box and withdraw the rocker. Reassembly is effected in the reverse order of dismantling.

Are Push-rod Covers Oil-tight? If any signs of oil leakage from the push-rod covers have been noticed, the rubber joint between the two halves of each telescopic cover should be scrutinized carefully. The rubbers for the inlet and exhaust push-rod covers must in any case be occasionally renewed, otherwise oil leakage is sure to occur. It is best to deal with one set of covers at a time to prevent the covers being interchanged, which is undesirable. To expose the rubber, push the bottom cover to the top of the upper cover. The rubber may then be removed or, if broken up, swilled out with clean paraffin. Slip the new rubber over the bottom cover into its proper position.

Final Reassembly (1935-6 S.V. Engines). After replacing the valves and cylinder barrel as previously described, wipe the joint faces of the barrel and head clean, put the piston at T.D.C. (both tappets down), lay the gasket on the barrel, refit the cylinder head, and tighten down securely and in a diagonal order the eight fixing studs. Then replace the exhaust pipe, carburettor, and plug after cleaning the two latter components (pages 6, 48). Replenish the oil "sump" if the crankcase has been drained (page 31) and adjust the tappets (page 45). Start up the engine and run it up gradually until oil circulation, as observed at the sight-feed window, is normal. Go out for a trial spin and note "the difference," which should be very marked.

Final Reassembly (1935-9 O.H.V. Engines). Cylinder barrel replacement has already been dealt with (page 74). Next refit the cylinder head gasket unless burnt or damaged, in which case it should be renewed. On the 1935-6 Models 50, 60, 90, 100 no gasket is required, but the metal-to-metal joint must be perfect. Discoloration implies gas leakage, the remedy for which is given on page 72. Now put the piston at T.D.C. with both tappets right down. Refit the cylinder head on the barrel, complete with rocker-box where these have been removed together, as explained in paragraphs (3) and (4) on page 62. First see that the rocker-box fixing bolts are tightened securely and that the rocker-box oil washers are in sound condition. Also pour a little oil into the wells around the valve springs. Tighten down firmly and in a diagonal order the bolts which secure the cylinder head, and in the case of the 1935-6 Models 50, 60, 90, 100 the barrel also. Where the rocker-box has not been removed together with the cylinder head, but separately as explained in paragraphs (2) and (5) on page 62, the cylinder head should first be replaced and then the rocker-box. On 1935-6 D.S. models with a cylinder head steady, replace the steady, but do not tighten the clip pin until *after* the head has been bolted down.

On the 1935-6 Models 70, 76, after refitting the cylinder barrel, insert the push-rods in the tunnels. Then place the push-rod joint face washer in position and lift the cylinder head on to the barrel spigot. Before bolting down the head, make sure that the push-rod joint face washer has not shifted and that the oil way in the centre of the washer is quite clear. To make certain, push a spoke or piece of wire down the hole. Now place the other push-rod joint face washer on top of the cylinder head and refit the rocker-box, together with its two oil-retaining washers. While doing this, be careful not to move the push-rod joint face washer.

On other engines with external push-rods, the push-rods and covers may be replaced after refitting the cylinder head and rocker-box and tightening down the bolts. To do this, use a screwdriver to compress the valve springs or, alternatively, the special tool referred to and illustrated on page 63. See that the push-rods engage the tappet heads and rocker-arm balls properly, and smear a little oil on their extremities. If the ends of the push-rods have worn much, replacement is necessary. Do not over-tighten the upper push-rod hexagon nuts (K, Fig. 35). Adjust the tappets or rocker screws (Models 50, 60) as described on page 45, after reconnecting the exhaust valve lifter (Models 50, 60). Finally replace the exhaust pipe(s), carburettor, and sparking plug, cleaning the latter before replacement (pages 6, 48). Reconnect the rocker-box feed pipe (where fitted), replace the petrol tank (if this has been removed), not forgetting to replace the rubber insulation buffers; and on 1937-9 engines with internal oil pumps, reconnect the extension of the rocker-box feed pipe to the oil indicator union. Replenish the oil "sump" or tank if the crankcase or tank has been drained (pages 27, 34), start up, watch the oil indicator or sight-feed (pages 27, 31) and, if all is well, go for a trial run. The engine should now have plenty of "snap."

THE SPRING FRAME

Many owners of 1937-9 models doubtless possess machines fitted with a spring frame (fitted as standard on certain models),

OVERHAULING

which gives delightful comfort even when traversing poor roads, and a few maintenance hints should prove useful.

Lubrication. Information on lubrication and an illustration showing lubrication points will be found on pages 41, 42.

Make Use of Damper. To obtain maximum efficiency and comfort, make full use of the damper D (Fig. 43). For fast road work, the damper should be tightened more than for travelling at a moderate speed. The same applies, of course, to the shock-absorber on the front forks, and with a little practice it is possible to work the two dampers in conjunction with each other to give the best results.

To Dismantle the Damper. If it is desired to dismantle the damper for inspection and, if necessary, renewal of worn parts, first remove the small aluminium disc C (Fig. 43) in the centre of the damper wheel D. Then remove the two nuts which hold the damper together by turning *anti-clockwise*. The damper wheel can now be removed, and the damper plates and friction discs withdrawn.

Adjustment of Spring Frame. To check the rear bearing for side play, slip a box beneath the crankcase so as to lift the rear wheel off the ground and then apply pressure sideways to the wheel; this should enable play to be readily detected. To take up side play, undo the lock-nut A (Fig. 43) on the main spindle by turning anti-clockwise, and then turn the knurled dust cap B *clockwise* until all play is eliminated. Do not employ any tool on the dust cap, as this is designed for hand adjustment. After making the necessary adjustment, retighten the lock-nut A securely.

At the base of the saddle stay tubes is a fulcrum pin E, provided to give freedom of movement at this point. The degree of movement of the stays about the fulcrum pin, however, is very small and slight side play which may develop is taken up by a fibre washer. After a considerable mileage it is desirable to remove the fulcrum pin E and examine the condition of the washer; if it shows signs of deterioration, fit a new one immediately. The fulcrum pin has an ordinary R.H. thread.

The Sprung Carrier. A sprung carrier (Fig. 43) is available as an extra for attachment to the spring frame. It is mounted at the front end on a lug H built into the saddle lug. Two stays J support the rear of the carrier, and both ends of the stays are

Fig. 43. Transmission Side of 1938-9 Model with Spring Frame and Carrier

OVERHAULING

pivoted on bosses *K*, *L*. Always see that the pivot pins are free enough to enable the carrier to move up and down, and that they are properly lubricated (page 43).

STEERING HEAD AND FRONT FORKS

Correct adjustment of the steering head and forks influences to a big extent the steering and general manoeuvrability. Friction due to inadequate lubrication attention has a detrimental effect.

FIG. 44. SHOWING METHOD OF DISMANTLING THE STEERING HEAD

Therefore a little regular maintenance is well worth while. For notes on lubrication, see page 41.

To Test for Play in Steering Head. The steering head should occasionally be tested for bearing play. Place some packing beneath the engine so as to take the weight off the front forks. Then after slackening the steering damper (where fitted), stand on the off-side, grip the centre of the ball-head clip with the left hand, and with the other hand attempt to push and pull the front wheel towards and away from the steering head. Any play present should easily be detected. Another method is to stand astride the machine and try and "shake" the handlebars. If adjustment is correct, it should be possible to move the handlebars left and right without the slightest trace of friction, and without there being any up-and-down movement. To take up steering head play, loosen the locking bolt on the steering head clip and screw down slightly the large adjuster nut.

Removing Steering Head Bearings for Inspection. As may be seen in Fig. 44, it is necessary to remove only the bottom fork spindles and links. First remove the steering damper anchor plate (where fitted) and the steering head nut, and then loosen the steering head locking bolt. The fork column can now be tapped out and removed as shown in Fig. 44. Be careful to see that none of the bolts are lost by dropping out when the forks are removed; hold the hand or a piece of paper below. Examine the ball races carefully and renew any races which are pitted. Also renew the balls if these are in questionable condition. Clean all parts with paraffin and, before replacing the bearings, pack the races with grease. Removal of the steering head for examination of the bearings is usually necessary only at long intervals, unless the machine has been run with slack bearings. It should be noted that the method of removal and dismantling, described above, obviates the necessity for disconnecting any handlebar controls or cables in the lighting system.

Steering Damper Use and Overhaul. A steering damper is fitted on all the faster models and is controlled by a knob on top of the fork column. To bring the damper into action, turn the knob *clockwise*. Generally speaking, the rougher the going and the higher the speed, the greater is the damping action needed, but on a sidecar outfit it is advantageous to have the damper in continuous use. After a very considerable mileage new friction discs or an anchor plate may be required due to wear, and the correct method of fitting is as follows.

Remove the steering damper knob and the rod passing down the steering column completely. Also remove the pin which secures the damper anchor plate to the front down tube. Now remove the weight from the front forks by putting some packing under the engine, and proceed to remove the *bottom* fork spindles as described previously. It will then be found that the steering damper assembly falls out complete, enabling the friction discs to be removed, examined, and, if necessary, renewed. If wear has occurred, a new anchor plate should be fitted. When re-assembling, the various parts should be replaced in the reverse order of removal.

Adjustment of Fork Shock-absorbers. Shock-absorbers are fitted on all 1938-9 models except lightweight machines with pressed-steel forks. Hand adjustment is provided except on some of the smaller models. Where hand adjustment is provided, the means of adjustment varies according to whether the shock-absorbers are of the single or double type. With single type shock-absorbers (used on most 1937-9 models and a few 1935-6 models), the spring action of the front forks is controlled by a shock-absorber hand disc mounted on the front top, or more usually the front bottom, fork spindle on the off-side. To damp the fork action and reduce spring rebound when travelling fast over poor road surfaces, the control disc should be turned *clockwise*. In the case of the double type shock-absorber, the fork action is controlled by two shock-absorbers on either side of the front bottom fork spindle, hand adjustment taking the form of two small levers. On 1938-9 models the hand adjustment is entirely independent of the spring fork adjustment and is made by turning the levers *clockwise*. On 1935-6 models, however, the double shock-absorber adjustment must be made in conjunction with the spring fork adjustment described below, except in the case of the 1935 "Grand Prix" models, where the adjustment is independent.

Adjustment of Forks (Pressed Steel Type). No adjustment is provided on this type of spring forks, as it is quite unnecessary.

To Adjust Forks (1935-6 Tubular Type without Shock-absorbers). The need for fork adjustment is usually indicated by a creaking noise on turning the steering sharply, and the play may often be felt. To take up side play, slacken the spindle nuts anti-clockwise and turn the bolt heads on the opposite ends of the spindles clockwise until all play is removed. While making the adjustment for each spindle, see that the spring action of the forks is not interfered with. Finally retighten the lock-nuts securely.

To Adjust Forks (1935-9 Single Shock-absorber Type). Should any side play develop, slacken the fork spindle nuts on the near-side anti-clockwise, and then turn the nuts inside the links clockwise until all side play is removed, afterwards retightening the outside nuts.

To Adjust Forks (1938-9 Double Shock-absorber Type). On the "Clubman" models side play may be taken up as follows. Slacken the spindle nuts by turning anti-clockwise and turn the spindles by means of their square ends anti-clockwise until play is removed. Afterwards retighten the spindle nuts. Each spindle should be adjusted separately and the forks should be tested for free action. The above adjustment also applies to the 1935 "Grand Prix" models.

To Adjust Forks (1935-6 Double Shock-absorber Type). Should side play develop, first slacken the fork spindle nuts on the near-side anti-clockwise and then turn the nuts inside the links clockwise until all side play is eliminated. Afterwards retighten the outside nuts.

The adjustment of the bottom front spindle is provided for by the tensioning of the shock-absorbers, and is the same as for the other spindles, except that the inside nut is held in position by two pegs on the fork link. These pegs must be disengaged in order to adjust the shock-absorbers by unscrewing almost completely the nuts on the bottom fork links on the near-side of the machine and tapping the link gently away from the inside adjusting nuts until the pegs are quite clear. To increase the effect of the shock-absorbers, turn the levers *clockwise*. Finally, replace the fork link, making sure that the pegs register with the holes in the adjusting nut; retighten the outside nuts.

Dismantling Shock-absorber (Single Type). In the centre of the adjustable hand disc is another small aluminium disc, which may be prised out in order to expose the two nuts which hold the shock-absorber together. Undo these anti-clockwise with a box spanner, and screw off the adjustable hand disc in the same direction, permitting the shock-absorber plates and friction discs to be removed. Clean the various parts and replace any which are worn. Replacements, however, should not be needed until after a big mileage. Reassemble in the reverse order of dismantling.

THE TRANSMISSION

Not much attention apart from lubrication (dealt with in Chapter III) is required to ensure smooth action of the transmission, consisting of the gearbox, the clutch, and the primary and secondary drives.

Adjustment of Foot Change (1935-9 Internal Type). The mechanism of the internal type foot change mechanism is shown in Figs. 20, 45. The unit is accurately set when assembled by the manufacturers, and it is almost impossible for it to get out of adjustment. To raise or lower the foot change lever to suit individual requirements on 1935-7 models, loosen the hexagon headed bolt which retains the lever on the splined operating shaft, slide the lever completely off, and replace on the desired spline, afterwards retightening the locking pin. On 1938-9 models there are two positions in the foot change operating lever to which is fitted the bottom yoke end. The inner position gives a harder

OVERHAULING 83

change with a minimum movement of the foot lever, while the outer position gives an easier change with a slightly longer movement.

Adjustment of Foot Gear Change (1935-6 External Type). It is

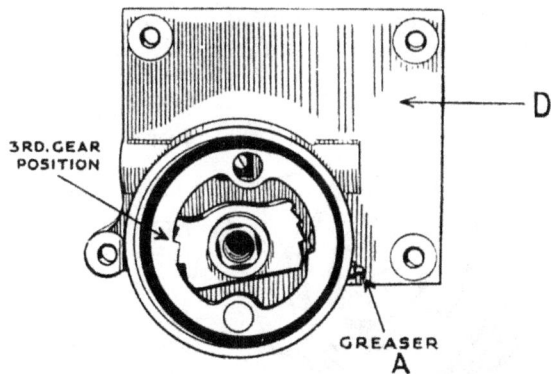

Fig. 45. Foot Change (Internal Type)

advisable occasionally to check the gear adjustment. This is best done when the front of the foot change is removed for greasing (page 38). Before dismantling, put the machine into *third gear*

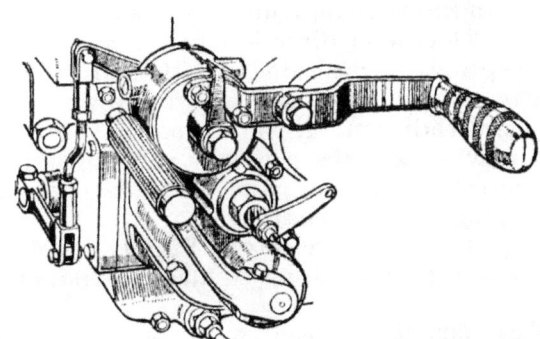

Fig. 46. Complete Foot Change Assembly (External Type)

A similar view of the complete internal type assembly is shown in Fig. 20. With the external and internal type units, to change up, raise or depress the foot pedal respectively.
(*From "The Motor Cycle"*)

position. Then remove the top yoke end pin from the **gear rod** (Fig. 46) and the front of the foot change as described on page 84. Fig. 46A shows the kick change in third gear, and all adjustments should be carried out in this position. If the selector arm of the gearbox is not in the correct third gear position, a slight touch up or down will cause the spring-loaded internal selector to engage the gear properly. Now attempt to replace the yoke end pin, which should slide into position freely if the hole in the selector arm registers with the holes in the yoke end. If, however, these holes do not register, adjust the length of the gear control rod by first slackening the small lock-nut at the top of the rod, adjusting the yoke end up or down until the desired position is found. Retighten the lock-nut, and replace the yoke end pin and split pin.

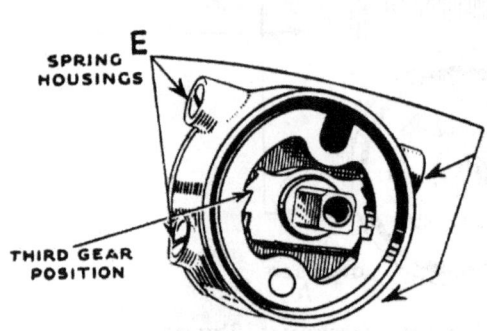

Fig. 46A. Foot Change (External Type)

To Replace Foot Change Springs. Four coil springs return the foot change lever to its normal position in the foot change mechanism, and after a big mileage the springs should be renewed if the lever tends to operate loosely or does not return to its central position.

To replace the foot change springs, first remove the gearbox lid *D* (Fig. 45) and foot change unit by unscrewing the four fixing bolts in an anti-clockwise direction. Four screwed caps *E* (Fig. 46A) hold the springs in position, two at the front of the unit and two at the rear. These caps should be unscrewed (anti-clockwise) and the springs withdrawn. If the springs have lost their tension, replace with new ones. Observe that the upper pair of springs are longer than the bottom pair. Replace the mechanism by carefully engaging the internal selector arm in the slot at the back of the glut or gear selector. Finally, screw in the four retaining bolts and do not forget to fit a new paper washer.

Gearbox Adjustment. In the event of any internal gearbox trouble developing, the author strongly advises the reader to remove the gearbox (where detachable) or take the complete machine along to the nearest well equipped garage for expert attention. Special tools are needed, and gearbox overhaul is not a job which should be undertaken except by those with plenty of experience. For this reason, gearbox overhaul will not be dealt with in this book.

To Adjust Gear Control (Hand Change). Should the primary chain (1935-6 models) be adjusted by moving the gearbox, or

OVERHAULING 85

the petrol tank be removed, the adjustment of the gear control should be checked.

Place gear lever into *second gear* position and remove the split pin and yoke end pin from the bottom yoke end. If the selector

FIG. 47. TRANSMISSION SIDE OF 1938-9 ENGINE
Showing helical gear-driven clutch and engine shaft shock-absorber. The primary drive cover is, of course, removed. A view of the timing side of this engine is given on page 64.

arm on the gearbox is not in correct second gear position, a slight touch up or down will cause the spring-loaded internal selector to engage the gear properly. Next, attempt to replace the yoke end pin—this should slide into position freely if the hole in the selector arm registers with the holes in the yoke end; if, however, these holes do not register, adjust length of gear control rod by first slackening the small lock-nut on the bottom of the rod, and adjust the yoke end up or down till the desired position is found. Retighten lock-nut and refit yoke end pin and split pin.

Is Clutch Adjustment Correct? Lack of backlash in the clutch cable will cause that most annoying of all transmission trouble—

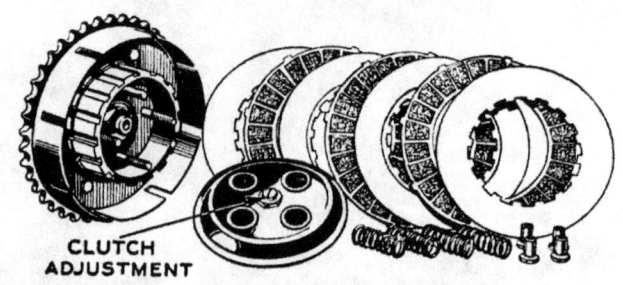

Fig. 48. 1935-6 Multi-plate Clutch Dismantled
This arrangement is provided on some models with D.S. lubrication. Note the adjustment on the spring plate.

clutch slip. With the clutch cable correctly adjusted there should always be about $\frac{1}{16}$ in. play at the handlebar lever. Should no play exist, slacken the lock-nut of the adjuster screw situated above the kick-starter housing and then turn the adjuster screw *anti-clockwise* until the correct adjustment is obtained. Afterwards retighten the lock-nut in the reverse direction. Similarly, if play is excessive, turn the adjuster screw *clockwise.*

In the case of the 1936 Models 90, 100, and 1935 "Grand Prix" Models 50, 60, a second clutch adjustment is provided. On removing the cover of the primary chain case, a lock-nut and slotted screw will be observed in the centre of the spring plate (Fig. 48). To increase or decrease the effective length of the clutch push rod, loosen the lock-nut and with a screwdriver screw in or out the adjuster screw. After making an adjustment, firmly retighten the lock-nut and replace the chain case cover.

Relining the Clutch. In order to reline the plates or fit new inserts, the clutch must, of course, be dismantled, but the clutch centre and back plate should not be disturbed. Instructions for dismantling the clutch in order to clean the plates (advisable occasionally) and, if necessary, reline them are given in succeeding paragraphs. On all the 1935-9 New Imperial models Ferodo

OVERHAULING

linings or Ferodo insert friction plates are employed. Relining is best done by the makers as this requires considerable skill.

To Dismantle Multi-plate Clutch (1935-6 Models 50, 60, 90, 100).
Remove firstly the primary chain case cover and then unscrew the four sleeve nuts from the spring plate (Fig. 48), and take out the springs and spring cups. Then withdraw the four plain plates and the three Ferodo insert plates. when reassembling start

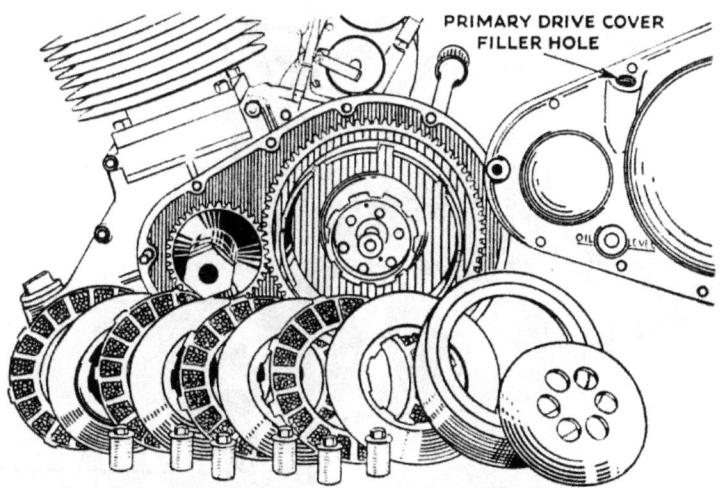

Fig. 49. 1935-6 Multi-plate Clutch Dismantled
Showing correct order of assembly on Models 70, 76, 80.

with a plain plate and finish with a plain plate. The correct order of assembly is clearly shown in Fig. 48. Finally refit the spring plate, insert the springs and cups, and tighten the four sleeve nuts fully. Replace the chain case cover after adjusting the clutch if necessary.

To Dismantle Multi-plate Clutch (1935-6 Models 70, 76, 80).
First remove the cover enclosing the helical gear drive and clutch. Then take out the six small pins from the outer spring plate (Fig. 49), and remove the springs and cups. The four Ferodo insert plates and the four plain plates may now be withdrawn. On reassembly, start with a friction plate and finish with a plain plate. See that all the dished plain plates, except the first one (nearest backplate) are replaced with the dished side *inwards*. The correct assembly order is shown in Fig. 49. After reassembling the plates, slip the ring cover right over the plates and afterwards replace the spring plate, spring cups, and springs. Retighten the six pins fully and finally refit the primary transmission cover.

88 BOOK OF THE NEW IMPERIAL

To Dismantle Multi-plate Clutch (1935-6 Models 30, 30DL, 35, 36, 37, 40, 45, 46, 47, 49, and 1937-9 Models 23, 36L). On this clutch the friction plates comprise two Ferodo discs, one behind and one in front of the large helical-toothed gear wheel, and two plates fitted with Ferodo inserts. The clutch centre back plate *C* (Fig. 50), with the gear wheel and rollers, should not be removed except by a competent mechanic, as there is an oil spinner washer driven by the six back plate stud nuts at the back of this plate.

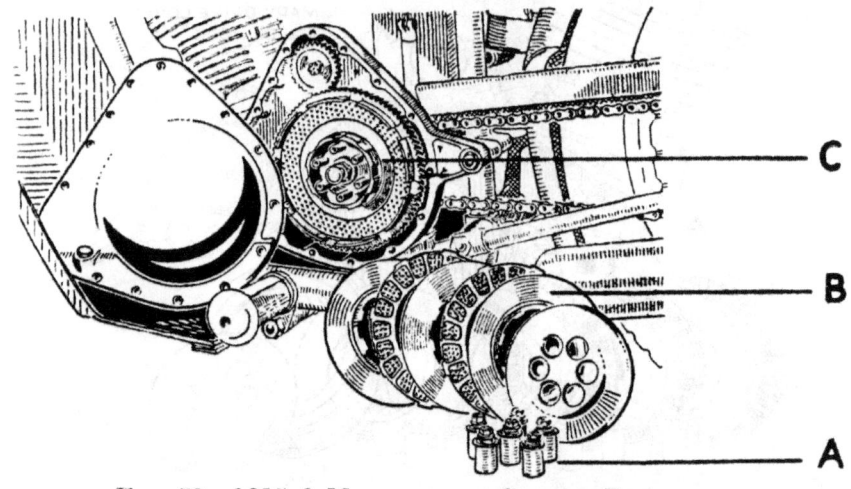

FIG. 50. 1935-9 MULTI-PLATE CLUTCH DISMANTLED
Provided on lightweight models where the dynamo (coil) or "Maglita" is gear-driven from the clutch.

These nuts must register correctly in the oil spinner wheel, otherwise serious damage to the primary transmission cover will be caused.

To dismantle the clutch after taking off the primary transmission cover, unscrew the six pins arranged around the outer spring plate, and withdraw the springs and spring cups *A* (Fig. 50). The clutch plates *B* may then be withdrawn. The correct order of reassembling the plates is shown in the illustration, and is as follows: (1) Ferodo disc, (2) one dished splined plate with the dished side outwards, (3) Ferodo insert plate, (4) flat splined plate, (5) Ferodo insert plate, (6) dished splined plate with the dished side inwards. Finally replace the outer clutch spring plate, spring cups and springs, and screw home fully the six pins. It then remains to refit the primary transmission cover.

To Dismantle Multi-plate Clutch (1937-9 Models 36, 46, 36DL, 46DL, and 1937-8 Model 90). Remove the primary transmission cover (see Fig. 47) and proceed exactly as described in the preceding paragraph. The correct order of reassembling the plates is also exactly as given above. See that the pins passing through the outer spring plate are retightened until right home, and finally replace the transmission cover.

To Dismantle Multi-plate Clutch (1937-9 Models 76, 76DL, 110, and 1937-8 Model 100). After removing the primary transmission cover (Fig. 47), proceed to remove the clutch plates exactly as described for the 1937-9 Models 23, 36L (page 88). Reassemble the plates in this order: (1) insert plate, (2) splined plate with dished side outwards, (3) insert plate, (4) splined plate with dished side outwards, (5) insert plate, (6) splined plate with dished side inwards. Replace the spring plate, spring cups and springs, and tighten fully home the six retaining pins, afterwards replacing the transmission cover.

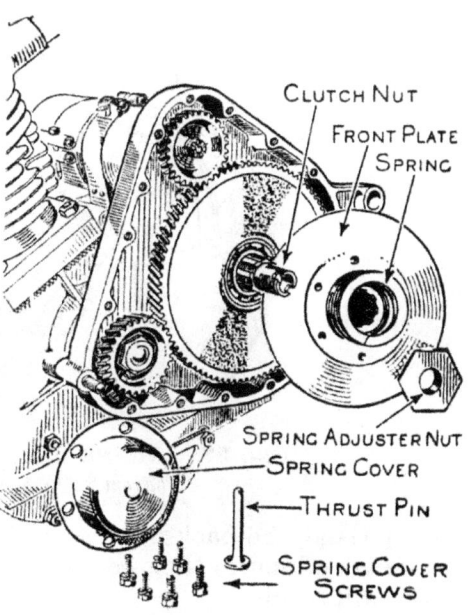

Fig. 51. 1935-6 SINGLE-PLATE CLUTCH DISMANTLED

A single-plate clutch with cork linings is fitted only on the 1935-6 lightweights.

To Dismantle Single-spring Clutch (1935-6 Models 23, 23DL, 25, 27). Cork linings are used on these machines and, as they run continuously in oil, replacement is seldom necessary. To dismantle the clutch, remove the transmission cover and unscrew the six clutch spring cover pins (Fig. 51). Then unscrew the large hexagon clutch spring adjuster nut anti-clockwise and withdraw the front plate. To avoid the necessity for having to retime the ignition, the small engine pinion and the dynamo or "Maglita" pinion should not be moved when the clutch gear wheel is removed.

The journal ball bearing, which is situated in the centre of the clutch gear wheel, is made a tight press fit, and should on no account be removed from the gear wheel. The centre portion of this journal bearing should slide quite freely on the splined centre of the clutch back plate, allowing it to be withdrawn complete with the gear wheel. Place new corks in position and carefully slide gear wheel back again; reassemble remaining parts in the reverse order in which they were dismantled. To facilitate the fitting of the spring, unscrew the clutch nut, by means of the slot, in an anti-clockwise direction until it is possible to start the clutch spring adjusting nut on the threads with the fingers—the whole then being locked up solid in a clockwise direction (see Fig. 51).

The clutch back plate should not be taken off except by a skilled mechanic, as there is an oil spinner washer driven by two

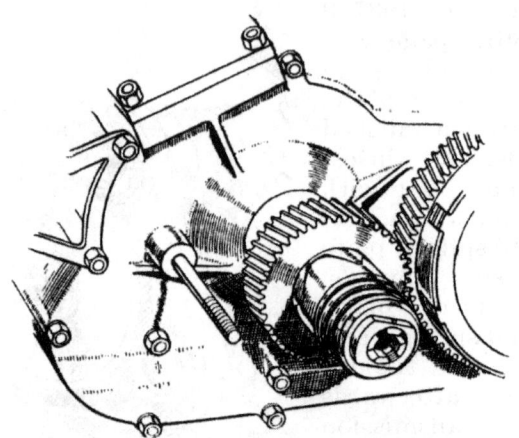

FIG. 52. ENGINE SHAFT SHOCK-ABSORBER
(*From "The Motor Cycle"*)

steel pegs at the back of this plate; these pegs must fit correctly in the oil spinner, otherwise serious damage to the primary drive cover will result.

The Engine Shaft Shock-absorber. An engine shaft shock-absorber of the face cam type (Figs. 47, 52) is provided on most 1935-6 and later models, except those where a "Maglita" or dynamo is gear-driven from the clutch gear. As may be seen in Fig. 52, the shock-absorber unit is mounted on the driving side main shaft, and comprises three inclined faces cut on the engine pinion which engage three similar faces on a sleeve. Both the sleeve and pinion are able to slide longitudinally, but must rotate with the engine. They are kept in engagement by means of a strong compression spring, which is adjustable for tension by turning the spring adjuster nut clockwise to increase the tension or anti-clockwise to decrease the tension. For notes on lubrication, see page 39.

To Dismantle Shock-absorber. First remove the split cotter securing the spring adjuster nut and remove the nut by turning

OVERHAULING

anti-clockwise. On close inspection, two lips on the shock-absorber lip washer (which have been knocked down into their locking position) will be noticed on top of the sleeve nut. With a chisel, knock these lips upright. Then replace the spring adjuster nut and insert a tyre lever or similar tool into the slot in the sleeve nut; grip the lever with an adjustable spanner and tap anti-clockwise with a hammer to remove the sleeve nut. Having removed the sleeve nut, pull off the engine pinion and the sleeve. The shock-absorber adapter may also be readily pulled off, as this is fitted on parallel main shaft splines.

On heavyweight models double helical gears are used, and in this case if it is desired to remove the engine pinion it is necessary to dismantle the clutch (page 88), and remove the engine pinion and the clutch gear together.

When reassembling, it is always necessary to fit a new lip washer and split cotter, as these are weakened during removal. Reassemble in the reverse order of dismantling, being careful to knock the lips on the locking washer well down into the slots provided (a special tool is obtainable from R. H. Collier & Co., Ltd).

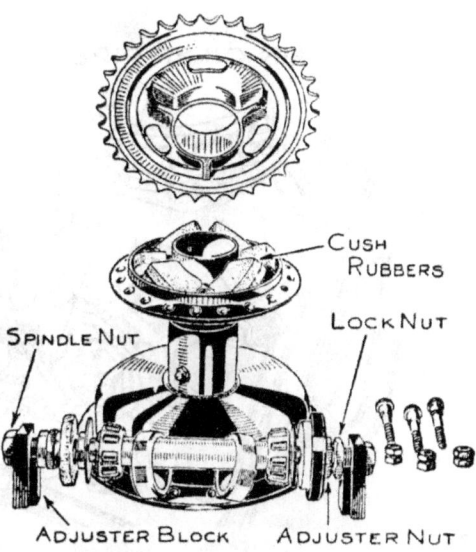

Fig. 52A. 1935-6 CUSH DRIVE REAR HUB

The Cush Drive Rear Hub. Many 1935-6 lightweight models (see page 40) incorporate a cush drive in the rear hub, details of which are shown in Fig. 52A. After a big mileage the rubbers will need renewing. To do this, remove the rear wheel (page 95) from the machine, and take off the spindle nuts and adjuster blocks (Fig. 52A). Then remove the large nut holding the brake anchor plate in position and pull the plate right off. Lightly tap the end of the spindle with a mallet. As the spindle comes away, it carries the dust cover and bearing from the cush drive end. Next remove the three bolts holding the sprocket in position by undoing the nuts (clockwise). Then pull off the sprocket. Referring to Fig. 52A, it will be noticed that the **rubbers are shown leaning on each other to enable the three segments on the sprocket to be inserted**

between the rubbers without trouble. As the sprocket is replaced, these rubbers automatically position themselves. Having refitted the sprocket, tighten home the three securing bolts together with their nuts and locking nuts. Finally, replace the spindle, being careful to lock tightly the nut securing the brake anchor plate.

Dismantling 1935-6 Models 70, 76, 80. The shock-absorber on these models is similar to that described above, but the engine

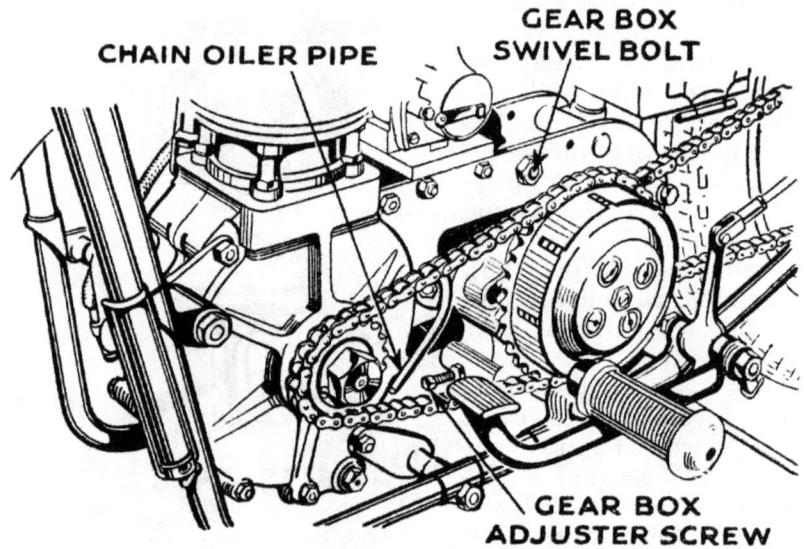

FIG. 53. 1935-6 PRIMARY CHAIN ADJUSTMENT
Observe also the chain oiler pipe (see page 35)

pinion and sleeve are carried directly on the engine main shaft instead of on a separate adapter. This method of construction avoids the necessity for a shock-absorber sleeve nut, double-lip washer, and split cotter. To dismantle the shock absorber, it is only necessary to unscrew the spring nut anti-clockwise and withdraw the spring and sleeve. Double helical gears are used on these models, and pinion removal necessitates simultaneous removal of the clutch gear.

Primary Chain Adjustment (1935-6 Models F10, F11, 50, 60, 90, 100). On these models with D.S. lubrication the primary chain is adjusted for tension by swivelling the gearbox backwards or forwards. After adjustment for tension has been made, it is necessary on models with hand-gear control to check the adjustment of the control, and also to check the tension of the rear chain. The tension of the primary chain is correct when the chain has

OVERHAULING

approximately ½ in. free up and down movement mid-way between the sprockets. On all other 1935-9 models, except those mentioned above, gear transmission is employed, and the question of slackness in the transmission does not arise.

To adjust the primary chain tension, slacken the nut on the gearbox swivel bolt (Fig. 53) and also the lower bolt. Then swivel the gearbox by means of the adjuster screws, one of which is shown in Fig. 53. In order to tighten the chain, loosen the

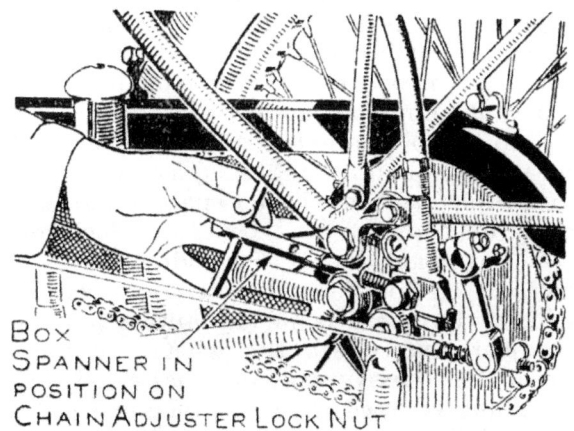

FIG. 54. USING BOX SPANNER TO ADJUST CHAIN TENSION

lock-nut and adjuster screw in front of the gearbox, and also loosen the rear lock-nut and turn the rear adjuster screw *clockwise*. The front adjuster screw should be loosened considerably before moving the rear one. When the correct chain tension has been obtained, firmly retighten the nut on the swivel bolt. Also tighten the footrest bolt and the front adjuster screw. Turn the latter *clockwise*. To slacken the chain, reverse the above instructions regarding the tightening and loosening of the gearbox adjuster screws.

Secondary Chain Adjustment (All Models). Whip in the secondary chain should not be allowed to develop as it presents a considerable element of danger. It is advisable to check the tension of the chain fairly frequently, as it runs at high speed and is rather exposed. The tension of the chain is correct when the chain has approximately ½ in. free up and down movement midway between the sprockets. Adjustment is effected by moving the rear wheel in the fork ends, and should be carried out as follows if it is desired to tighten the chain.

The back spindle nuts (see Fig. 54) in the fork ends should be loosened on each side by turning left-hand. The two chain adjuster pins, which pass through the solid portion of the fork end, and press against the adjuster block on the spindle, should now be turned right-hand, but before doing this the small lock-nut should be loosened by turning left-hand, so as to allow the pin to move inwards. This has the effect of pushing the wheel backwards and farther from the gearbox, consequently tightening the chain. It is very important that both these chain adjuster pins should be turned exactly to the same extent, not one more than the other, as if this is not carried out the alignment of the transmission will be detrimentally affected, and may lead to much trouble. When the correct tension of the chain has been obtained, the small lock-nut should be locked up to the solid portion of the fork end, so as to retain the adjuster pins in their correct position, the two spindle nuts tightened as before, and the adjustment is then complete. A small box spanner will be found in the tool kit for use on chain adjuster pins and lock-nut. It will be found that the box spanner (Fig. 54) slides over the head of each adjuster bolt and on to the lock-nut. When testing the chain tension, see that the chain is in its tautest position and, after making an adjustment, check the wheel alignment (page 98). If it is necessary to remove a chain, make sure on replacing it that the spring link is fitted with the open end facing *away from* the direction of chain motion. Chain lubrication is dealt with on page 40.

BRAKES, WHEELS, AND TYRES

Always keep the brakes in perfect adjustment if only on the grounds of safety, the wheel bearings properly adjusted, and the tyre pressures correct. Brake and hub lubrication have already been dealt with in Chapter III.

Brake Adjustment. Hand adjustment for both brakes is provided on some models, but in the majority of cases there is hand adjustment for the rear brake only. Adjustment is needed to take up the normal wear of the shoe linings. To adjust the front brake, it is only necessary to take up play in the cable by means of the hand adjuster (where fitted) or the lock-nut and cable stop adjuster on the front brake anchor plate (Fig. 25). Make sure that the adjustment is not overdone, causing the brake shoes to bind. To take up play in the rear brake, a wing nut is provided at the end of the brake rod (Fig. 54). Turn the wing nut clockwise to counteract wear of the brake shoe linings and afterwards see that the wheel spins freely. Should the linings become greasy, remove the shoes and clean the linings with petrol. The remedy for linings which become polished and lose their efficiency is to

OVERHAULING

clean them with petrol and then roughen them with a stiff bristle brush or a file. Scored brake drums should be returned to the makers for attention.

To Remove Front Wheel (All Models). Place the machine on the front stand or, in the case of some lightweight models where no stand is fitted, raise the wheel from the ground by placing a small box under the crankcase. Now remove the front brake

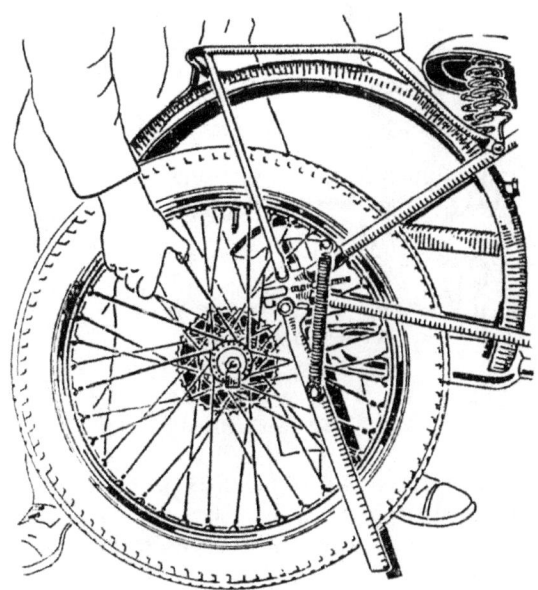

FIG. 55. REMOVING REAR WHEEL
The rear tyre should be deflated if necessary.

cable at the handlebar end by holding the brake operating lever (on the hub) with a spanner, which will allow sufficient slack in the cable for the cable end cap to be removed from the handlebar lever. Next slacken both spindle nuts (anti-clockwise) and withdraw the wheel. When replacing the wheel, see that the brake anchor plate is correctly positioned on the stud, and that the spindle nuts are firmly retightened and the brake cable adjusted if necessary.

To Remove Rear Wheel (All Models). Jack the machine up on the rear stand and, where the rear half of the back mudguard is detachable, remove the tail piece. Unscrew the brake rod wing nut and anchor plate stop pin. Also remove the spring connecting link from the rear chain. Now slacken both wheel spindle nuts and pull the wheel from the fork ends as shown in Fig. 55, leaning the machine over on its near-side to assist removal where a detachable tail piece is not fitted. To replace the wheel, again lean the machine to the near-side, if necessary, and lift the wheel into position in the fork ends. Be sure that the chain adjuster blocks are fitted correctly in their slides with the portion of the block which fits into the fork end *to the rear*. Replace the chain and screw the brake anchor plate stop pin into position so that

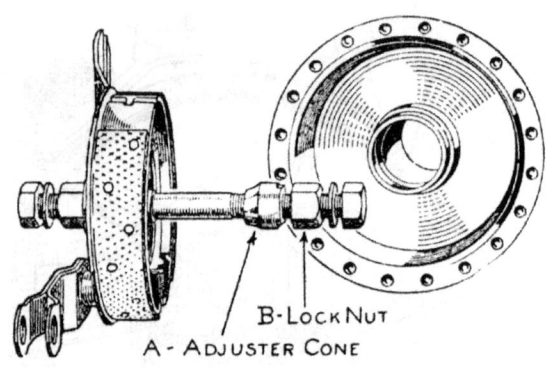

Fig. 56. Front Hub Adjustment
(Ball bearing type.)

the end of the pin enters the slot. Next retighten the spindle nuts and reconnect the brake rod. Finally, refit the mudguard tail (if removed), check wheel alignment (page 98), and see that the chain tension is correct (page 93).

Is Wheel-bearing Adjustment Correct? It is advisable occasionally to check the wheel bearings for play by grasping each wheel around the tyre and attempting to "shake" the wheel. In the case of ball-bearing hubs, *no* play should exist, but the wheel must be free to revolve without any friction. With roller-bearing hubs fitted to all except some of the lightweight models, there should be $\frac{1}{32}$ in. play *measured at the rim*. It is of vital importance that such side play exists where roller bearings are concerned. The correct method of adjusting the wheel bearings on the various models is described in the following paragraphs.

To Adjust Front Hub Bearings (1935-6 Models 23, 23DL, 25, 27, 30, 30DL, 35, 37, 40, 45, 47, 49, and 1937-9 Models 23, 36, 36L, 46). Slacken lock-nut *B* (Fig. 56) anti-clockwise and adjust cone *A* clockwise to take up play in ball bearings. Then tighten lock-nut *B*, being careful to see that cone *A* is not shifted, otherwise the adjustment will be spoiled.

OVERHAULING

To Adjust Rear Hub Bearings (1935-6 Models 23, 23DL, 25, 27, and 1937-9 Models 23, 36, 36L, 36DL, 46, 46DL). Slacken lock-nut C (Fig. 57) and then adjust the taper roller bearings by means of the nut D. Afterwards retighten lock-nut C.

To Adjust Front Hub Bearings (1935-6 Models 36, 46, 70, 76, 80, F10, F11, 50, 60, 90, 100. 1937-9, 36DL, 46DL). Referring to Fig. 58, to adjust for side play in the taper roller bearings, slacken

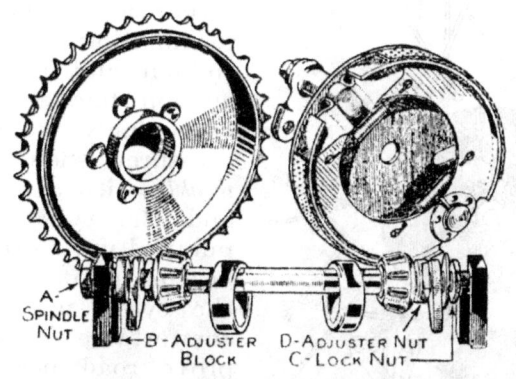

FIG. 57. REAR HUB ADJUSTMENT

the lock-nut A (anti-clockwise) and then turn the taper roller bearing B in a *clockwise* direction if it is desired to take up play, or *anti-clockwise* if it is necessary to increase the play. Afterwards retighten lock-nut A.

To Adjust Front Hub Bearings (All 1937-9 Models except Models 23, 36, 36L, 46). Follow exactly the instructions given in the previous paragraph. A view of the front hub assembly is shown in Fig. 58.

To Adjust Rear Hub Bearings (1935-6 Models 36, 46, 70, 76, 80, F10, F11, 50, 60, 90, 100). Referring to Fig. 59, to take up play in the taper roller bearings, slacken the lock-nut C anti-clockwise and turn the adjuster nut D *clockwise*. Afterwards retighten the lock-nut C and, when the job is complete, test for play.

To Adjust Rear Hub Bearings (All 1937-9 Machines except Models 23, 36, 36L, 36DL, 46, 46DL). Referring to Fig. 59, follow exactly the instructions given in the previous paragraph.

To Adjust Rear Hub Bearings (1935-6 Models 30, 30DL, 35, 37,

40, 45, 47, 49). To adjust the taper roller bearings in the rear hub, which on these machines incorporates a cush drive (see Fig. 52A), slacken the lock-nut and turn the hexagon adjuster nut which forms part of the dust cover. After making the necessary adjustment, retighten the lock-nut.

Use Correct Tyre Inflation Pressures. Running on incorrectly inflated tyres may not produce any immediate ill-effects, but in the long run it causes serious deterioration of the tyre casings, terminating perhaps in a sudden and unexpected concussion burst which may be exceedingly dangerous. Tyre pressures should be checked *weekly* with a gauge (Fig. 62) and the tyres, if necessary, pumped up. Correct pressures, besides giving a fair deal to the tyres, provide the most comfortable riding and improve road performance to a small extent. Under-inflation, it may be mentioned, sets up internal casing strains, which cause ultimate cracking of the casing. Over-inflation also strains the casing and makes punctures more likely; it also sets up undue vibration. The table on page 101, reproduced by courtesy of the Dunlop Rubber Co., Ltd., shows correct inflation pressures for Dunlop tyres.

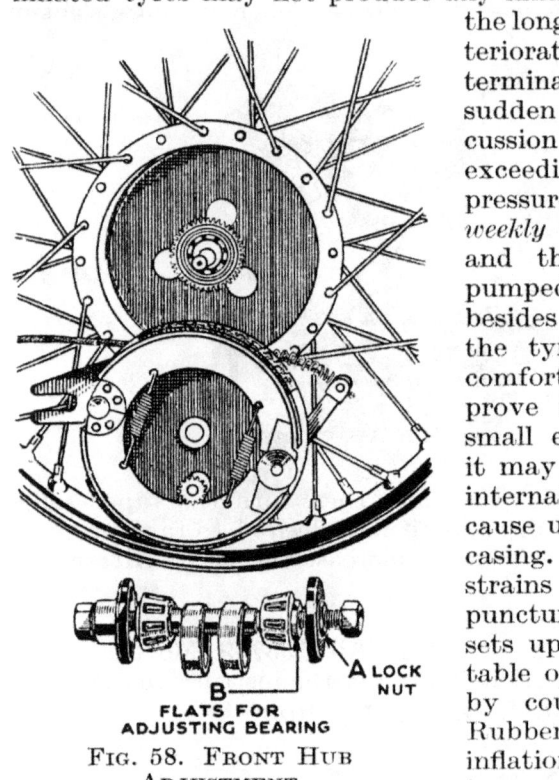

FIG. 58. FRONT HUB ADJUSTMENT
A LOCK NUT
B FLATS FOR ADJUSTING BEARING

Is Wheel Alignment Correct? It is extremely important to keep the front and rear wheels perfectly aligned, otherwise tyre wear is rapid and uneven, and the machine is likely to develop a skidding "complex." Proper alignment of the third wheel on a sidecar outfit is also most important. If the steering becomes uncertain and a tyre shows more wear on one side than the other side, test the alignment. The rear chain adjusters may have been *unequally* adjusted. To test the alignment on a solo machine, place a straight edge or a taut piece of string alongside the two wheels (Fig. 60), and turn the front wheel until the straight edge or string touches both sides of the front tyre and one side of the rear tyre. If the wheels are correctly aligned, it will also touch the other side of the rear tyre. To rectify faulty alignment, alter the position of the rear wheel spindle by means of the fork adjusters.

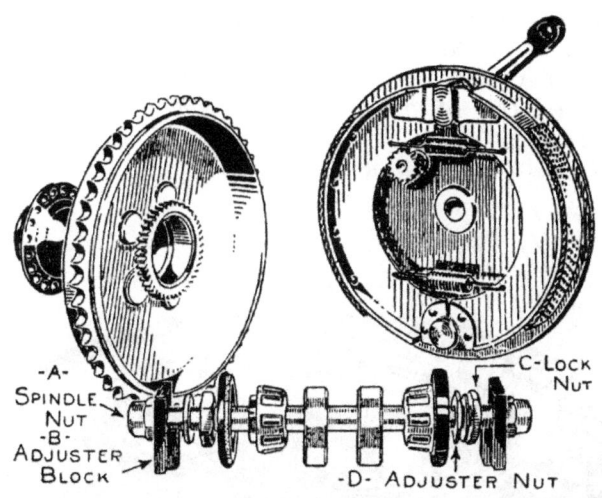

Fig. 59. Rear Hub Adjustment

In the case of a sidecar machine, align the motor cycle wheels as described above, and then place another straight edge across the sidecar tyre and note if the two edges are parallel. They

Fig. 60. How to Check Wheel Alignment on a Solo

should be nearly so, but not quite. There should be a slight "toe in" at the front to the extent of about $\frac{1}{2}$ in. The motor cycle should be vertical.

Repairing Tubes (Non-synthetic). To prevent punctures, keep the inflation pressures correct and examine the tyres weekly for cuts and embedded flints. When removing a cover with tyre levers in order to repair the tube, commence near the valve and push the opposite side of the tyre cover into the base of the rim (see Fig. 61). To locate the puncture, submerge the tube in water. Then clean the vicinity of the puncture with fine sandpaper and rub off all dust. Now select a suitable size auto-vulcanizing patch, such as the "Vulcafix," and detach its linen backing. If solution is not used, rub the prepared side of the

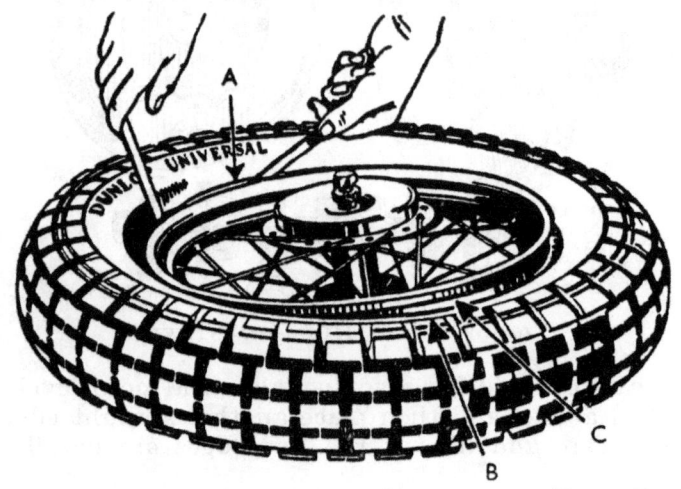

Fig. 61. Correct Method of Removing a Tyre Cover
(*Dunlop Rubber Co. Ltd.*)

Remember that tyre beads are inextensible, and, before attempting to lever the cover bead at *A* over the flange of the wheel rim, ease the cover bead at *B* off the rim shoulder *C* down into the well.

patch with a petrol-moistened cloth and transfer the brown deposit on the cloth to the seat of the puncture. Repeat this procedure and permit the transferred deposit and patch to dry for one minute. Where solution is employed, apply this to the *tube only* and wait for it to become "tacky." Finally, affix the patch to the tube, using slight pressure, especially round the edges, and apply french chalk to prevent adherence of the tube to the cover.

Repairing Synthetic Tubes. GR-S synthetic tubes can be recognized by a 1 in. diameter red disc or stripe. The following points should be noted in connection with their repair. Preferably all punctures or damage should be vulcanized, but it is satisfactory to make an emergency repair of small holes or tears up to $\frac{1}{4}$ in. Use a "Vulcafix" or similar auto-vulcanizing patch,

OVERHAULING

and make sure that the tube is first thoroughly roughened and solutioned before attempting to apply the patch. Take the tube to a competent repairer for vulcanizing if the injury exceeds ¼ in.

Dunlop Tyre Inflation Pressures (Lb. per Sq. In.)

Tyre Section (In Inches)	16	18	20	24	28	32
	Load per tyre (Fully Laden) in lb.					
2·375	120	140	160	185	210	240
2·50	120	140	160	185	210	240
2·75	140	160	180	210	250	280
3·00	160	180	200	240	300	350
3·25	200	240	280	350	400	440
3·50	280	320	350	400	450	500
4·00	360	400	430	500	—	—

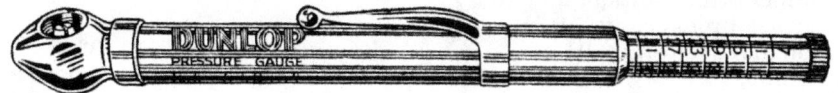

Fig. 62. A Convenient Pressure Gauge—The Dunlop Pencil Type No. 6

Is Your Plug Waterproof. It is a good plan (if you do much all weather riding) to fit a watertight plug or a waterproof terminal cover on the existing plug. Lodge insulated shock-proof terminal covers are available at 1s. 6d., and a waterproof K.L.G. terminal (which clips on K.L.G. plugs) can be obtained for 2s. A range of waterproof K.L.G. plugs is also available. The type Nos. for these plugs have the prefix "W" (e.g. WF70).

Spares and Accessories. Should you require any spares for your New Imperial, Messrs. R. H. Collier & Co., Ltd. (see Preface) can probably fix you up. When ordering, *always* quote the engine and frame numbers. The firm mentioned will undertake a rebore if necessary.

Five large firms (with many branches) which can supply a great variety of motor-cycle accessories, tools, clothing, etc., are: The Halford Cycle Co., Ltd.; Marble Arch Motor Supplies; George Grose, Ltd.; Turners Stores; James Grose, Ltd.

INDEX

ADJUSTMENTS, running-in, 44
Air filter, 12
Amal carburettor, 1–12
Ammeter, 18

BATTERY maintenance, 19
Brake adjustment, 94
Brushes, dynamo, 14
Bulb replacements, 21

CARBURETTOR, 1, 8
Charging, 19
Clutch, 86–90
Commutator, 16
Compensated voltage control, 17
Contact-breaker, 49–54
Cush drive rear hub, 91
Cut-out, 17
Cylinder, removing, 61–5

DECARBONIZING, 61–9
Dry-sump lubrication, 33–6
Dynamo maintenance, 13, 36, 52

ENGINE oils, 23
Exhaust valve lifter, 46

FOCUSING, 21
Foot change, 38, 82–4
Fork spindles, 41, 81

GEARBOX adjustment, 84
—— lubrication, 37–9
Generator drive, lubrication of, 37
Greases, suitable, 37
Grinding cylinder head to barrel, 72
Grinding-in valves, 71

HAND gear change, 39, 84
Hub lubrication, 42

IGNITION timing, 55–9

LAMPS, 20
Lubrication, 23–43

"MAGDYNO" chain adjustment, 55
—— maintenance, 13, 36, 49
"Maglita" maintenance, 37, 54

PETROL tank removal, 61
Piston removal, 65
—— rings, 66–8
Primary transmission, 39, 92

REASSEMBLY, engine, 74–6
Running-in, 23, 44

SECONDARY chain, 40, 93
Semi-dry-sump lubrication, 24–33
Shock absorber, engine, 90
—— ——, fork, 80, 82
Slow running, 6
Sparking plug, 47–9, 101
Speedometer drive, 43
Spring frame, 42, 76–9
Starting, 11
Steering damper, 80
—— head, 41, 79

TAPPET adjustment, 44–6
Topping-up battery, 19
Tyres, 98–101

VALVE clearances, 44–6
—— timing, 59
Valves, reassembling, 73
——, removing, 69–71

WARNING lamp, 54
Wheel alignment, 98
—— bearings, 42, 96–8
—— removal, 95–6
Wiring diagram, 22

AUTOBOOKS WORKSHOP MANUALS

ALFA ROMEO GIULIA 1300, 1600, 1750, 2000 1962-1978 WSM
BMW 1600 1966-1973 WSM
BMW 2500, 2800, 3.0 & 3.3 1968-1977 WSM
BMW 316, 320, 320i 1975-1977 WSM
BMW 518, 520, 520i 1973-1981 WSM
FIAT 1100, 1100D, 1100R & 1200 1957-1969 WSM
FIAT 124 1966-1974 WSM
FIAT 124 SPORT 1966-1975 WSM
FIAT 125 & 125 SPECIAL 1967-1973 WSM
FIAT 126, 126L, 126 DV, 126/650 & 126/650 DV 1972-1982 WSM
FIAT 127 SALOON, SPECIAL & SPORT, 900, 1050 1971-1981 WSM
FIAT 128 1969-1982 WSM
FIAT 1300, 1500 1961-1967 WSM
FIAT 131 MIRAFIORI 1975-1982 WSM
FIAT 132 1972-1982 WSM
FIAT 500 1957-1973 WSM
FIAT 600, 600D & MULTIPLA 1955-1969 WSM
FIAT 850 1964-1972 WSM
JAGUAR MK 1, 2 1955-1969 WSM
JAGUAR S TYPE, 420 1963-1968 WSM
JAGUAR XK 120, 140, 150 MK 7, 8, 9 1948-1961 WSM
LAND ROVER 1, 2 1948-1961 WSM
MERCEDES-BENZ 190 1959-1968 WSM
MERCEDES-BENZ 220/8 1968-1972 WSM
MERCEDES-BENZ 220B 1959-1965 WSM
MERCEDES-BENZ 230 1963-1968 WSM
MERCEDES-BENZ 250 1968-1972 WSM
MERCEDES-BENZ 280 1968-1972 WSM
MINI 1959-1980 WSM
MORRIS MINOR 1952-1971 WSM
PEUGEOT 404 1960-1975 WSM
PORSCHE 911 1964-1973 WSM
PORSCHE 911 1970-1977 WSM
RENAULT 16 1965-1979 WSM
RENAULT 8, 10, 1100 1962-1971 WSM
ROVER 3500, 3500S 1968-1976 WSM
SUNBEAM RAPIER, ALPINE 1955-1965 WSM
TRIUMPH SPITFIRE, GT6, VITESSE 1962-1968 WSM
TRIUMPH TR4, TR4A 1961-1967 WSM
VOLKSWAGEN BEETLE 1968-1977 WSM

VELOCEPRESS AUTOMOBILE BOOKS & MANUALS

ABARTH BUYERS GUIDE
AUSTIN-HEALEY 6-CYLINDER WSM
AUSTIN-HEALEY SPRITE & MG MIDGET 1958-1971 WSM
BMW 600 LIMOUSINE FACTORY WSM
BMW 600 LIMOUSINE OWNERS HAND BOOK & SERVICE MANUAL
BMW 2000 & 2002 1966-1976 WSM
BMW ISETTA FACTORY WSM
CARRERA PANAMERICANA - MEXICAN ROAD RACE (BOOK OF)
COMPLETE CATALOG OF JAPANESE MOTOR VEHICLES
CORVAIR 1960-1969 OWNERS WORKSHOP MANUAL
CORVETTE V8 1955-1962 OWNERS WORKSHOP MANUAL
DIALED IN - THE JAN OPPERMAN STORY
FERRARI 250/GT SERVICE AND MAINTENANCE
FERRARI 308 SERIES BUYER'S AND OWNER'S GUIDE
FERRARI BERLINETTA LUSSO
FERRARI BROCHURES AND SALES LITERATURE 1946-1967
FERRARI BROCHURES AND SALES LITERATURE 1968-1989
FERRARI GUIDE TO PERFORMANCE
FERRARI OPP, MAINTENANCE & SERVICE H/BOOKS 1948-1963
FERRARI OWNER'S HANDBOOK
FERRARI SERIAL NUMBERS PART I - ODD NUMBERS TO 21399
FERRARI SERIAL NUMBERS PART II - EVEN NUMBERS TO 1050
FERRARI SPYDER CALIFORNIA
FERRARI TUNING TIPS & MAINTENANCE TECHNIQUES
HENRY'S FABULOUS MODEL "A" FORD
HOW TO BUILD A FIBERGLASS CAR
HOW TO BUILD A RACING CAR
HOW TO RESTORE THE MODEL 'A' FORD
IF HEMINGWAY HAD WRITTEN A RACING NOVEL
JAGUAR E-TYPE 3.8 & 4.2 WSM
LE MANS 24 (THE BOOK THAT THE FILM WAS BASED ON)
MASERATI BROCHURES AND SALES LITERATURE
MASERATI OWNER'S HANDBOOK
METROPOLITAN FACTORY WSM
MGA & MGB OWNERS HANDBOOK & WSM
MG MIDGET TC, TD, TF & TF1500 WORKSHOP MANUAL
OBERT'S FIAT GUIDE
PERFORMANCE TUNING THE SUNBEAM TIGER
PORSCHE 356 1948-1965 WSM
PORSCHE 912 WSM
SOUPING THE VOLKSWAGEN
SOLEX CARBURETORS (EMPHASIS ON UK & EU AUTOMOBILES)
SU CARBURETORS (EMPHASIS ON UK AUTOMOBILES)
TRIUMPH TR2, TR3, TR4 1953-1965 WSM
TUNING FOR SPEED (P.E. IRVING)
VEDA ORR'S NEW REVISED HOT ROD PICTORIAL
VOLKSWAGEN TRANSPORTER, TRUCKS, STATION WAGONS WSM
VOLVO 1944-1968 ALL MODELS WSM
WEBER CARBURETORS (EMPHASIS ON ALFA & FIAT)

VELOCEPRESS THREE WHEELER BOOKS & MANUALS

BSA THREE WHEELER (BOOK OF)

BROOKLANDS BOOKS & ROAD TEST PORTFOLIOS (RTP)

AC CARS 1904-2009
ALFA ROMEO 1920-1933 ROAD TEST PORTFOLIO
ALFA ROMEO 1934-1940 ROAD TEST PORTFOLIO
BRABHAM RALT HONDA THE RON TAURANAC STORY
BUGATTI TYPE 10 TO TYPE 40 ROAD TEST PORTFOLIO
BUGATTI TYPE 10 TO TYPE 251 ROAD TEST PORTFOLIO
BUGATTI TYPE 41 TO TYPE 55 ROAD TEST PORTFOLIO
BUGATTI TYPE 57 TO TYPE 251 ROAD TEST PORTFOLIO
DELAHAYE ROAD TEST PORTFOLIO
FERRARI ROAD CARS 1946-1956 ROAD TEST PORTFOLIO
FIAT 500 1936-1972 ROAD TEST PORTFOLIO
FIAT DINO ROAD TEST PORTFOLIO
HISPANO SUIZA ROAD TEST PORTFOLIO
HONDA ST1100/ST1300 PAN EUROPEAN 1990-2002 RTP
JAGUAR MK1 & MK2 ROAD TEST PORTFOLIO
LOTUS CORTINA ROAD TEST PORTFOLIO
MV AGUSTA F4 750 & 1000 1997-2007 ROAD TEST PORTFOLIO
TATRA CARS ROAD TEST PORTFOLIO

VELOCEPRESS MOTORCYCLE BOOKS & MANUALS

1930'S BRITISH MOTORCYCLE CARBS & ELEC COMPONENTS (BOOK OF)
1930'S BRITISH MOTORCYCLE GEARBOXES & CLUTCHES (BOOK OF)
AJS SINGLES & TWINS 250cc THRU 1000cc 1932-1948 (BOOK OF)
AJS SINGLES 1955-65 350cc & 500cc (BOOK OF)
AJS SINGLES 1945-60 350cc & 500cc MODELS 16 & 18 (BOOK OF)
ARIEL 1939-1960 4 STROKE SINGLES (BOOK OF)
ARIEL LEADER & ARROW 1958-1964 (BOOK OF)
ARIEL MOTORCYCLES 1933-1951 WSM
ARIEL PREWAR MODELS 1932-1939 (BOOK OF)
BMW M/CYCLES R26 R27 (1956-1967) FACTORY WSM
BMW M/CYCLES R50 R50S R60 R69S (1955-1969) FACTORY WSM
BSA BANTAM ALL MODELS FROM 1948 ONWARDS (BOOK OF)
BSA SINGLES & V-TWINS UP TO 1927 (BOOK OF)
BSA SINGLES & V-TWINS UP TO 1935 (BOOK OF)
BSA SINGLES & V-TWINS 1936-1939 (BOOK OF)
BSA SINGLES & V-TWINS 1936-1952 (BOOK OF)
BSA OHV & SV SINGLES 250-600cc 1945-1954 (BOOK OF)
BSA OHV & SV SINGLES - 250cc 1954-1970 (BOOK OF)
BSA OHV SINGLES 350 & 500cc 1955-1967 (BOOK OF)
BSA TWINS 1948-1962 (BOOK OF)
BSA TWINS 1962-1969 (SECOND BOOK OF)
CATALOG OF BRITISH MOTORCYCLES (1951 MODELS)
DOUGLAS PRE-WAR ALL MODELS 1929-1939 (BOOK OF)
DOUGLAS POST-WAR ALL MODELS 1948-1957 FACTORY WSM
DUCATI 160cc, 250cc & 350cc OHC MODELS FACTORY WSM
HONDA 50 ALL MODELS UP TO 1970 INC MONKEY & TRAIL (BOOK OF)
HONDA 90 ALL MODELS UP TO 1966 (BOOK OF)
HONDA MOTORCYCLES 125-150 TWINS C/CS/CB/CA WSM
HONDA MOTORCYCLES 250-305 TWINS C/CS/CB WSM
HONDA MOTORCYCLES C100 SUPER CUB WSM
HONDA MOTORCYCLES C110 SPORT CUB 1962-1969 WSM
HONDA TWINS & SINGLES 50cc THRU 305cc 1960-1966 (BOOK OF)
HONDA TWINS ALL MODELS 125cc THRU 450cc UP TO 1968 (BOOK OF)
INDIAN PONYBIKE, BOY RACER & PAPOOSE ILL PARTS LIST & SALES LIT
J.A.P. ENGINES 1927-1952 & MOTORCYCLES 1934-1952 (BOOK OF)
LAMBRETTA ALL 125 & 150cc MODELS 1947-1957 (BOOK OF)
LAMBRETTA LI & TV MODELS 1957-1970 (SECOND BOOK OF)
MATCHLESS 350 & 500cc SINGLES 1945-1956 (BOOK OF)
MATCHLESS 350 & 500cc SINGLES 1945-1966 (BOOK OF)
MOTORCYCLE ENGINEERING (P. E. Irving)
NEW IMPERIAL ALL SV & OHV 1935 ONWARDS (BOOK OF)
NORTON 1932-1947 (BOOK OF)
NORTON 1938-1956 (BOOK OF)
NORTON DOMINATOR TWINS 1955-1965 (BOOK OF)
NORTON MODELS 19, 50 & ES2 1955-1963 (BOOK OF)
NORTON MOTORCYCLES 1957-1970 FACTORY WSM
NORTON PREWAR MODELS 1932-1939 (BOOK OF)
NSU PRIMA ALL MODELS 1956-1964 (BOOK OF)
NSU QUICKLY ALL MODELS 1953-1963 (BOOK OF)
PANTHER HEAVYWEIGHT MOTORCYCLES 600 & 650cc (BOOK OF)
PANTHER LIGHTWEIGHT MOTORCYCLES 250 & 350cc (BOOK OF)
RALEIGH MOPEDS 1960-1969 (BOOK OF)
RALEIGH MOTORCYCLES 1919-1933 (BOOK OF)
ROYAL ENFIELD SINGLES & V TWINS 1934-1946 (BOOK OF)
ROYAL ENFIELD SINGLES & V TWINS 1937-1953 (BOOK OF)
ROYAL ENFIELD SINGLES 1946-1962 (BOOK OF)
ROYAL ENFIELD 736cc INTERCEPTOR FACTORY WSM
ROYAL ENFIELD 250cc & 350cc SINGLES 1958-1966 (SECOND BOOK OF)
RUDGE MOTORCYCLES 1933-1939 (BOOK OF)
SPEED AND HOW TO OBTAIN IT
SUNBEAM MOTORCYCLES 1928-1939 (BOOK OF)
SUNBEAM S7 & S8 1946-1957 (BOOK OF)
SUZUKI 50cc & 80cc UP TO 1966 (BOOK OF)
SUZUKI T10 1963-1967 FACTORY WSM
SUZUKI T20 & T200 1965-1969 FACTORY WSM
TRIUMPH PRE-WAR MOTORCYCLE 1935-1939 (BOOK OF)
TRIUMPH MOTORCYCLES 1935-1949 (BOOK OF)
TRIUMPH MOTORCYCLES 1937-1951 WSM
TRIUMPH MOTORCYCLES 1945-1955 FACTORY WSM
TRIUMPH TWINS 1945-1958 (BOOK OF)
TRIUMPH TWINS 1956-1969 (BOOK OF)
VELOCETTE ALL SINGLES & TWINS 1925-1970 (BOOK OF)
VESPA 1951-1961 (BOOK OF)
VESPA 125 & 150cc & GS MODELS 1955-1963 (SECOND BOOK OF)
VESPA 90, 125 & 150cc 1963-1972 (THIRD BOOK OF)
VESPA GS & SS 1955-1968 (BOOK OF)
VILLIERS ENGINE UP TO 1959 INC. 3 WHEELERS (BOOK OF)
VILLIERS ENGINE UP TO 1969 (BOOK OF)
VINCENT MOTORCYCLES 1935-1955 WSM

For complete details of any title please visit our website www.VelocePress.com

Please check our website:

www.VelocePress.com

for a complete up-to-date list of available titles

www.ingramcontent.com/pod-product-compliance
Lightning Source LLC
Chambersburg PA
CBHW070559170426
43201CB00012B/1882